MALAYSIAN CUSTOMS & ETIQUETTE

A Practical Handbook

Datin Noor Aini Syed Amir

TIMES BOOKS INTERNATIONAL
Singapore • Kuala Lumpur

Selected photographs by courtesy of
Jabatan Penerangan Malaysia.

© **1991 Times Editions Pte Ltd**

Published by Times Books International
an imprint of Times Editions Pte Ltd
Times Centre
1 New Industrial Road
Singapore 1953

Times Subang
Lot 46, Subang Hi-Tech Industrial Park
Batu Tiga
40000 Shah Alam
Selangor Darul Ehsan
Malaysia

Reprinted 1991, 1993, 1995

Printed in Singapore

ISBN 981 204 255 5

To all my "children"
especially Ean, Baby Amir,
and my own Afzan

CONTENTS

FOREWORD

I am indeed pleased to be given the opportunity to say a few words in this practical handbook, *Malaysian Customs and Etiquette*.

Malaysia is a country of fascinating and diverse attractions with a rich cultural heritage. It has so much to offer both to the local as well as foreign visitors of its indigenous cultural heritage and abundant natural resources. This compact and practical handbook will provide valuable insight of our multi-racial and multi-religious country.

As we continue to celebrate our "Visit Malaysia Year", I would like to congratulate Times Books International for their efforts in publishing this book.

DATO' SABBARUDDIN CHIK
Minister of Culture, Arts and Tourism
Malaysia

INTRODUCTION

Malaysia is a multi-racial country consisting predominantly of three races: the Malays or Bumiputera (Sons of the Soil), the Chinese and the Indians. Although the multi-racial aspect may not in itself be anything unusual, the unique feature here is that these three ethnic groups can live side by side (and they have been doing so for a long time now) yet still keep their own separate and individual identities.

The Bumiputera people form the largest ethnic group of Malaysia. Since the Bumiputera are considered the original people of Malaya, a heavier emphasis has always been placed on Bumiputera traditions, culture and etiquette. This is still the case today.

Bumiputera groups consist of the Malays (originally from the Northern Plains of Asia), the Orang Asli (the aborigines), and the Malay-related people. The Malay-related people come from the neighbouring Indonesian islands. Also in this category are the Bajau people of Sabah.

Malay-related people are considered Bumiputera because they share a common racial background and, above everything else, because they practise the same religion (Islam) as the Malays of the Malay Peninsular.

There is also a non-Malay Bumiputera category which consists of ethnic groups found in Sabah and Sarawak. These non-Malay Bumiputera people are basically of the same racial stock and they are considered the indigenous people of the region (North Borneo).

Non-Bumiputera groups consist primarily of the Chinese and the Indians. Much smaller communities of Arabs and Eurasians also exist.

Islam, brought primarily by Indian and Arab traders in the thirteenth century, became the major religion of the Malays when the mighty rulers of Melaka adopted it as their religion. It has thus played a predominant role in shaping Malay society and the Malay way of life.

The Chinese and Indians came as immigrants in the nineteenth century. Economic development was very rapid in Malaya during that period. In the sixteenth century, the Portuguese and later the Dutch arrived. Inter-marriage between the Europeans and the non-Muslim people of Malaya, especially in Melaka, resulted in a unique ethnic group called the Eurasians. The Eurasians today mostly embrace the Roman Catholic faith, they carry Portuguese or Dutch surnames and have become an important minority with the biggest community still found in Melaka. The other Eurasians of Malaysia are the first generation offspring from marriages between a Malaysian and a European: for example, the child of a Malay father and an English mother. The British Occupation (after the Second World War) brought a significant amount of Western influence into Malaya.

Malaysian culture today is a healthy mix of five distinct cultures – its own indigenous culture as well as Islamic, Chinese, Indian and Western cultures. As a Malaysian, I can safely say that we are very proud to have such a rich and unique blend of traditions and cultures. There may be countless things to observe, but this is what makes us truly the people of Malaysia: a people from different ethnic, religious and cultural backgrounds who *all* have a healthy respect for each other.

At this stage I would like to point out that I myself am of the Malay (Bumiputera) stock. The reader will note that I identify myself as such at various times throughout the book. I did this as a way of speaking for and on behalf of the Malay race on certain matters which applied more specifically to this particular ethnic group than to the other ethnic groups found in Malaysia. At other times I did this because I could speak with all certainty for the Malay people but did not feel

I had the right to speak for the non-Malays. It is not my intention to offend anyone when I repeatedly identify myself as a Malay.

The foreigner who has to live in Malaysia would be rather unrealistic if he felt he could live in a country such as this without having a little knowledge of its local customs and etiquette. This book then is an attempt to provide the foreigner with *basic but important* guidelines when living in (or visiting) Malaysia. This book is not a detailed, in-depth study of the traditions and/or cultures of the main ethnic groups in Malaysia. There are many books written specifically about these topics. Mine is not one of them.

My main aim is to give the foreigner a simple, easy-to-carry, easy-to-understand book which provides handy and useful information about the Malaysian way of life and how the foreigner is to behave and respond in various situations *without* going into too detailed or complicated an explanation.

First of all, I introduce some important Malaysian customs and provide a basic guide to table manners. Next, short explanations of major religious and cultural festivals are given with tips on appropriate gifts and dress for these festivals. Events such as births, birthdays, marriages and funerals are also discussed. Suggested gifts and appropriate dress for these occasions are given. Finally, I discuss in greater detail the proper forms of address. This is of great importance to the foreigner because Malaysia has a most complex system of titles! The foreigner would do well to know some of them by heart as he would need this knowledge in his day-to-day mingling with the Malaysian people.

It is my sincere hope that this book will answer most of the foreigner's questions regarding Malaysians as a whole.

If I have omitted anything or have committed any errors, I take all blame and would like to apologise for this. On the other hand, if I could make half my readers happy, then my sincere attempt at helping them has been truly worthwhile for me!

ACKNOWLEDGEMENTS

My sincere and heartfelt thanks to the following for their numerous suggestions, invaluable information, support and assistance.

Ambassador Datuk Abdullah
Syed Amir Abidin ibni Tuanku Syed Putra Jamalullail
Mrs Anita Abdul Aziz
Mrs June Lim
Ms Christine Chong
Mrs Vasantha Chandra
Mrs Geeta Peri
Mr Ahmad bin Hassan
Mr Md Yasin bin Sunyit

The photograph of a long-sleeved batik shirt on page 36 is reproduced by kind permission of Ambassador Datuk Abdullah and His Excellency Sir David Gilmore. I would also like to extend my gratitude to members of my family who have graciously allowed me to use their personal photographs. Extra special thanks go to my cousins Ee and Joe for a very special photograph: their Bersanding Ceremony. All other photographs are reproduced by kind permission of Jabatan Penerangan Malaysia.

1 SOME IMPORTANT MALAYSIAN CUSTOMS

The Malays

While the Malays are very generous and forgiving with foreigners who make Malay *faux pas*, those who do not make such blunders will be highly admired and respected.

Here are some guidelines to follow when in the presence of the Malays.

Upon visiting Malay homes

The first thing you would probably notice is that all Malaysians will take their shoes off before entering a Malay house. The reason for this is that when we perform our prayers with our guests, we usually do this in the living room. Therefore, should we wear our shoes inside, the shoes would soil the living room floor, making it unsuitable for prayers (we Muslims pray on a mat laid out on the floor).

Your Malay host would probably insist that you leave your shoes on, as foreigners are not really expected to follow this Malay custom. Should you, however, insist that you take them off, your action will be very much appreciated.

You will also note that this custom is true for the Chinese-Malaysians, Indian-Malaysians, and the Eurasian-Malaysians as well. More often than not, my non-Malay Malaysian friends take off their shoes before entering their own houses or the houses of their non-Malay friends.

Introductions Malay style have no hard-and-fast rules but you will notice that, with the Malays, age takes precedence over almost everything else, i.e. a younger Malay person would very likely make the first move to *salam* an older Malay person's hand.

The Malay handshake (*Salam*)

Unlike the Western handshake, which is a rather vigorous up and down movement where both parties grip the other's hand firmly, the Malay handshake is a simple palm-to-palm touch. Sometimes, only the fingertips brush against each other. The important part of this gesture is the bringing of the hand (one or both) back to the heart or the lower part of the face – the nose and mouth. This signifies that your greeting has been accepted with sincerity.

I have often heard the Western press describing some of our leaders as having a limp handshake. This is not the case; they are just giving a Malay handshake.

Also, sometimes the *salam* would only happen between people of the same sex. Always assuming that people are ready for prayers (i.e. they have performed their ablutions which forbids touching people of the opposite sex, unless closely related *by blood*), the touching of the palms would mean they would have to inconvenience the other person into taking his ablutions (*air sembahyang*) again.

The Malay handshake (*Salam*)

Some do's and don'ts

The head (from the bottom of the neck up) is considered sacred in Eastern culture. Foreigners please remember that under *no* circumstances should you touch the head of your Malaysian friend without permission. Even if you see an insect on your friend's head, it is best that you let him/her know about it rather than attempt to remove the insect yourself! An affectionate gesture like a pat on the head (even to a child) should also be avoided.

I remember visiting a hairdressing salon once where the hair-stylist asked my forgiveness first before touching my head, even though, under those circumstances, the touching of another person's head was obviously something that had to be done. Yes, the question of head touching can be that serious!

Is kissing allowed/acceptable among members of the opposite sex who are *not* married or related to each other?

Please, please approach this act with caution! Note that such an act of intimacy is *not* common among some Malay people and that such an action on your part may cause a lot of unnecessary embarrassment. Assess the situation thoroughly before you offer your cheek or you yourself lean forward to place a kiss on the cheek of your Malay friend. Please do not be offended if your Malay friend moves away (especially if he/she is of the opposite sex from you) but simply try to accept that this *can* be an alien tradition which some Malays will not accept for religious or cultural reasons.

The usual Malay way when entertaining people of both sexes is that the men will be invited to sit together and the ladies will be invited to sit together, i.e. the opposite sexes are segregated. It may seem strange to a foreigner but this is the way of life here in Malaysia. The more modern Malays would probably do away with this sort of segregation but even these more modern Malays would most likely bow down to tradition when their guests consist of the older generation.

Alternatively, a hostess may only segregate the older

Malay ladies and gentlemen and leave the younger ones to mingle with each other.

For the more traditional functions (e.g. a traditional birth or a traditional wedding) people are invited to sit on the floor. Although there are no rules for the men, foreign ladies please note that the following are *not* the correct ways of sitting down in a Malay house:

- with your legs crossed
- with your legs placed straight in front of your body
- squatting

The proper way of sitting (Malay style) is as follows: you would sit with your two legs neatly tucked against your seated body (left or right side is fine) with the feet facing *away* from people (as much as possible). If you can some-how manage it, tuck your feet *under* the hem of your dress.

The correct way of sitting on the floor

If you have brought a present with you to give to your Malay hostess, don't be disappointed if she puts it aside and leaves it unopened. We have always been taught not to open gifts in the presence of the person who gave it to us.

We only open our gifts when we are alone. Could it be that in doing it this way we spare the present giver the embarrassment of seeing the dismay on our face should the gift be less than what was expected? But seriously, I think it has something to do with modesty on the part of the receiver; whether good or not, we are indicating that the present has been received with thanks and whatever is inside the package takes second place to the thought that went behind it.

Should you wish to point at anything (you would probably want to do this during a wedding ceremony) you would use your thumb and not your forefinger. The correct way of doing this is to make a soft fist with your right hand. Place your thumb directly above this fisted hand. Only then do you point.

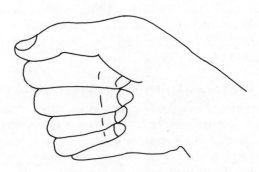

Pointing with the thumb

If you can help it, never ever use your left hand in Malay company! Foreigners may well be puzzled as to why the left hand cannot be used. The reason lies in tradition. It is a Malay custom that we wash ourselves each time we defecate and the left hand is used for this. Symbolically then, the left hand is considered unclean. Therefore, for all manner of gestures such as waving or pointing where only one hand is needed, only the right hand is used.

Even if you find yourself in a very modern Malay home with very modern people, please bear in mind that crossing the legs at the knees is considered rude in front of older Malay people and is absolutely forbidden in front of senior Malay royalty!

If you wish to send a note of thanks to the hostess the next day, by all means do so. Little gifts or a bouquet of flowers are quite acceptable.

The Non-Malays

The fact that I have gone to rather great lengths to discuss some important Malay customs in detail does not mean that the other ethnic groups have done away with their own traditions and culture. Far from it. Using the same guidelines as I did under the section on Malay customs, following are some tips for the foreigner when in the presence of their non-Malay Malaysian friends.

Upon visiting non-Malay homes

The foreigner already knows the reasons why we take our shoes off before we enter a Malay home. It has also been mentioned that this custom is true for the non-Malays as well. Though it may not be for religious reasons, the question of cleanliness is probably the issue here. As the Malays would appreciate it if a foreigner were to observe this particular custom, so would the non-Malays.

Segregation of the sexes exists primarily in Malay homes but it is fairly safe for me to say that Malaysian women (indeed most Asian women) often feel more at home in the presence of other women than they would with men, especially foreign men. This is even more so with women who were brought up following traditional Eastern teachings.

Indian women, in particular, are still highly conservative (especially the unmarried ones) and it is very likely that they would sit separately from the men at Indian functions.

Gestures of greeting

Handshaking between the different sexes for non-Malays is something that is dictated more by culture than religion. I am told that handshaking is not really a common practice with the Chinese-Malaysians (just a smile and a nod will do). Neither is it very widely used within the Indian-Malaysian groups, whose usual greeting is the palm to palm gesture (as in prayer): the two palms, touching each other, are brought to chest level and the head is bowed downwards towards the palms. (Please see the illustration below.) In general, handshaking is an acceptable form of greeting.

The Indian gesture of greeting

The important point here is this: whatever race one happens to belong to, respect for elders is of utmost importance! From the time we are able to understand, it has been instilled in us that, no matter what should happen, we *never* forget our manners towards people older than we are! Rudeness towards older people is a social offence considered intolerable in Malaysia, as it is throughout the rest of the Eastern world!

Therefore, whether by tradition, race, religion, or culture, a Malaysian person is always expected to greet an older person in the appropriate fashion. When we enter a Malaysian home, it is customary for us (if we happen to be younger) to greet all the older people first. It is not proper for us to wait for the older people to come to us and greet us.

Some do's and don'ts

The question of kissing (in greeting/farewell) between a foreigner and a Malaysian (non-Muslim) is something that should be left to the situation one finds oneself in. Because of conservative upbringing, one does not have to be of any particular race or religion to shy away from such an action. If your Malaysian friend is relatively broad-minded and is fairly exposed to Western culture, then a casual kiss is bound to be perfectly alright. However, if you take into consideration all the other aspects of Eastern culture and upbringing, your discretion is called upon before you kiss the cheek of your Malaysian friend.

Although not terribly particular as to how one should sit on the floor, to the Chinese, kneeling is simply not done except for the following two reasons:
1. if one is in the act of prayer, or
2. if one is in the act of asking for forgiveness.

For other than these two reasons kneeling is considered degrading and the person kneeling can suffer "loss of face" – a fate that the Chinese (the world over) would not wish for, except perhaps on their worst enemies!

The Foreigner Is Host

Food that is taboo

I feel very strongly that people, in general, should be sensitive towards religious and cultural beliefs of other people. While I am not asking the foreigner to embrace the religious laws and cultural traditions of the country he finds himself living in, I think the foreigner should, nevertheless, be aware of certain things. In Malaysia, food is one such thing. When a hostess plans her dinner menu, she must have her guest list within reach. If she has invited Malays, she must take care not to serve pork. If she has invited Indians, she must find out whether they are vegetarians or not, and so it goes on.

Malays are almost automatically Muslims too. As Muslims, Malays are only allowed to eat food that is *halal*. *Halal*, which means "permissible according to Muslim law", describes meat of animals slaughtered for food in the manner prescribed by Muslim law. Thus, *halal* describes lawful food. The closest equivalent in Western terms would be "Kosher" (which describes products that meet the requirements of Jewish law).

One of the things a Muslim is forbidden to eat by religious laws is pork – in any form or shape! While a Malay would not dream of imposing on his/her hostess and would probably sit very quietly through a dinner that included pork, I feel that it is totally unforgivable on the part of the hostess (especially since she already knows) to subject her Malay guest to such discomfort.

If you are inviting Indians, find out if they are Indian-Muslims. If they are not, chances are they would be Hindus, which could very probably mean they are vegetarians. Non-vegetarian Hindus do not eat beef (the cow is a sacred animal in Hinduism). Some Chinese too may be vegetarians and many others may abstain from mutton and/or beef.

How would a foreigner cater for all these different needs? My advice is to give priority to those foods that are forbidden by religious laws (e.g. pork and beef) and serve a variety of other foods which include lots of vegetables, chicken, and fish. The vegetarians will be happy and the non-beef, non-mutton eaters can eat the chicken and the fish.

The different types of food required at any one meal is probably the main reason why buffet lunches and dinners are more popular than sit-down dinners here in Malaysia. With a buffet, the hostess can lay out any amount and practically any type of food she wants. With a sit-down dinner, she is somewhat limited in her choice.

If it is a sit-down dinner a foreigner is organising, I would suggest inviting not more than a dozen people. In this way, a certain amount of control can be exercised when planning the menu.

The other thing that a foreigner has to be aware of is the serving of alcohol. This is a *very* sensitive issue – one that I would not even dare to begin to discuss! Suffice it for the foreigner to know that alcohol is *haram* (forbidden) to Muslims. Whether or not she (the hostess) wants to serve it to her non-Muslim guests is left to her own discretion.

Language problems

Do try to find out whether there is going to be a language problem among your guests. While most Malaysians speak English, you may find that those of the older generation or those that come from a traditional family may speak only Bahasa Malaysia. If your guest-of-honour (or his wife) falls into this category, do take the trouble to find someone who can keep this gentleman (or lady) happy throughout the evening. Time and time again I have personally seen the wife of a V.I.P. sitting through a dinner looking terribly forlorn because neither one of her two neighbours is able to converse in Bahasa Malaysia. Although you may have to go slightly against protocol in order to place a person who can speak the language next to this important lady, once you explain (discreetly) to the person you had to displace the reasons behind your move, I am sure he or she would not take offence.

2 TABLE MANNERS

Eating with Fingers

Malays and Indians traditionally use the fingers of their right hand for eating. However, no one expects a foreigner invited to a local-style meal (no cutlery) to be an expert at eating with fingers! Nevertheless, below are some useful guidelines to follow when you find yourself in a situation where using your fingers is the *only* way to eat:

1. Always remember to wash your hands first. If you are invited to a Malay wedding (or any other celebration) you will find a water vessel (*kendi*) either at your table or being passed around for guests to wash their hands. (Please refer to the illustration that follows.)

2. Meals are *always* eaten with your right hand! Being left-handed is no excuse.

3. Even though you are eating with your fingers, you will find that serving spoons are provided for all the dishes being laid out. Since the fingers of your right hand will be soiled while eating, you are permitted to use your left hand when using the serving spoons, although we always say "excuse me" (*minta maaf*) first.

4. When it comes to dessert, you may well find that you still have to use your fingers. Since dessert eaten with the fingers is usually dry, do wash your hands before starting your dessert. If it is some sort of pudding with a sauce or syrup, spoons will definitely be provided. You would wash your hands at the end of a meal using the *kendi* again.

Since the *kendi* has to be passed round from person to person, the polite thing to do is to wash your hands using a minimum amount of water! Personally, I do not find this very satisfying! Therefore, I always go out armed with a large supply of wet tissues (the ones packed for babies are ideal) which of course makes me the most popular person at the table when I begin to pass them around!

The other thing a foreigner should be made aware of is that it is *not* considered impolite for a person to leave the table once he has finished his meal. In many of the larger households (the same can apply during meals at big functions), a person leaves the table as soon as he is done so that he can give way to the other people waiting to eat.

A Kendi

A   The pot which holds the water.

B   The stand has holes in it for the water to filter through.

Washing Your Hands:

1. Lift the pot with your left hand and place your *right* hand (the hand you *must* use for eating) below it, above the stand.

2. Lightly rinse your hand with the water from the pot, making sure the water filters through the holes in the stand.

3. Replace the pot onto the stand.

Eating nasi daun pisang

Traditionally, Southern Indians eat off banana leaves. A variety of food including curries, vegetables and sauces are placed around a pile of rice. Dessert is usually served onto the same banana leaf after the main meal. To indicate that you have finished your meal, you fold your banana leaf in half. Some Indians say that if it is for a festive occasión (wedding) or if the food is very good, you fold the banana leaf *towards* you. If it is for a sombre occasion (funeral) or if the food is less than satisfactory, you fold the banana leaf *away* from you. This action may differ from clan to clan.

At the end of the meal, you have to get up to wash your hands as there will be no *kendi* (as at Malay meals) passed around.

Eating with your left hand or with cutlery is discouraged.

The banana leaf is usually divided into three pieces. The honoured guest gets the end piece (no. 3 – in the diagram).

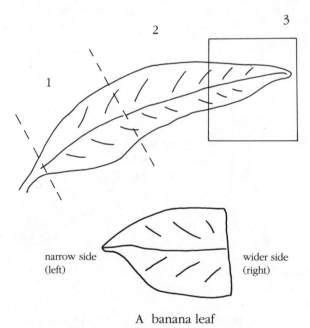

narrow side (left)

wider side (right)

A banana leaf

When placed in front of the guest, the narrow side is placed on the left, the wider side on the right. The reason the banana leaf is placed in this manner is so that the right side (as you eat with your right hand) will have more food.

Eating with Chopsticks

No matter what anybody has to say about this matter, I feel that you cannot thoroughly enjoy a Chinese meal unless you know how to handle the chopsticks!

Unlike at Malay meals, left-handers are allowed to use their left hand.

(Please refer to the illustration below for the proper way of holding chopsticks.) Two things to remember are: the bottom chopstick *always* remains stationary. The top chopstick is the one that makes all the different moves and is the one used to manoeuvre your food from the plate or bowl to your mouth. The bottom chopstick simply supports the top chopstick's movements, thus providing the grip.

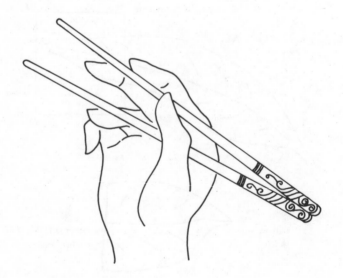

The proper way of holding chopsticks

Before your host or hostess has begun eating, he or she may first pick choice pieces with his or her own chopsticks to give to you. This is a way of showing that you are an honoured guest. For those who are very health-conscious, an extra pair of chopsticks may be used just for this purpose.

Chopsticks should *never* be crossed.

Neither should they be stuck vertically into your rice (placed in a small bowl) or any other food so that they resemble joss-sticks.

The end of the chopsticks which should be put in your mouth should be pointing *away* from you when you put them down or place them on their holder or stand. How would a foreigner know which end of the chopsticks is the end that enters the mouth? Well, the narrower or slightly tapered end is the one that goes inside your mouth!

Chopsticks may or may not be changed for clean ones during the meal but you will definitely get a different pair for dessert.

Unlike at Western meals, where there is a definite indication when your meal is finished, with a Chinese meal there are no hard-and-fast rules. It is best to place your chopsticks back onto the holder (or stand) or leave them on the side of your plate.

Would you bring your bowl of rice to your mouth or would you lean forward to bring your head towards the bowl which remains on the table? Traditionally, I am told that the first gesture (i.e. bringing the bowl to the mouth) is acceptable. What is *not* acceptable is to loudly slurp and suck the rice into your mouth. The correct way would be to use your chopsticks to transfer the food from the bowl to the mouth, even if the distance is minimal!

Eating with Fork and Spoon

Traditionally, the Malays and Indians would eat their food using their fingers and the Chinese would eat theirs using their chopsticks. However, for a long time now, especially in public eating places (hotels and restaurants) Western cutlery has appeared in most Malaysian table settings.

We have, however, slightly adapted the actual laying out of the cutlery as well as the use of certain utensils to suit our needs.

The rice spoon is one such utensil that is probably only found in Southeast Asian countries (i.e. Singapore, Malaysia, Thailand, Indonesia, and the Philippines). We are all rice eaters and we tend to build around our rice, i.e. the rice is our staple dish to which we would then add curries, sauces, vegetables and other dishes. We certainly do not feel a fork is the proper utensil to use for eating rice! By the time the rice reaches our mouth, more than half would have slipped through the tines of the fork. This certainly will not do. Instead, we use a rice spoon. The rice spoon is about the size of a dessert spoon. It is not as large as a serving spoon nor is it round like a soup spoon. It is placed on the right side of your plate. You would eat the rice as you would your dessert, holding the spoon in your right hand and your fork in your left hand. The rice should be scooped onto the spoon.

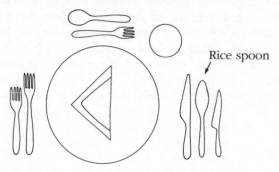

Rice spoon

Localised Western-style dinner setting

If you are invited to a Malay or Indian house where food would normally be eaten with the fingers, you may find that your glass will be placed next to the top *left* side of your plate, rather than on the right. This is for practical reasons only: if you eat with your right hand (which would then be soiled), it is only logical that you hold your glass in your left (clean) hand.

As a concession to your being a foreigner, a fork and spoon may be provided for you but your glass would probably remain on the left. Having already said that I doubt a Chinese meal could be thoroughly enjoyed unless you can actually manoeuvre your chopsticks properly, a foreigner can still eat Chinese food with the aid of spoons.

You will probably find two types of spoons already on the table. The first is a long silver spoon and the second is a short spoon which can be used to scoop up anything from soup to chili sauce. When in difficulty, a foreigner would be excused if he used either one of these two spoons to help him along.

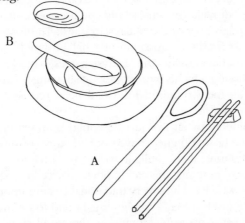

Chinese dinner table setting

A. Long silver spoon

B. Short spoon – very versatile. Can be used to help you with your rice or to scoop up any of the more difficult dishes.

Common Embarrassing Situations

People from the East (Asians as well as Arabs) have never been very rigid about table manners. Although children are taught basic discipline when they are facing their food, our table manners are nowhere near those to which our Western counterparts are accustomed.

Some of the most embarrassing situations that tend to arise time and time again are the conflicting gestures (Western gestures as opposed to Eastern ones) of how appreciation of food is shown.

To a person from the East, burping at the end of a meal shows that he had truly enjoyed his food and was most satisfied with it. And how else can one enjoy one's soup unless it is enthusiastically slurped into the mouth?

Anyone who has been exposed to Western culture will know that the two gestures described above are considered both rude and terribly unbecoming and should *never ever* be done in decent surroundings.

In the event that either one or the other (or both) should happen, I don't know who would end up more embarrassed – the foreign host or the Malaysian guest. The foreign host would obviously be appalled at what he would consider barbaric behaviour, and the Malaysian guest would probably be wondering why his two attempts at showing his appreciation of all the wonderful food had been received by the wrong response.

Admittedly, what I've just described is an extreme case where the host and guest have not had any exposure to the other's culture at all. Still, it would be advisable for the foreigner to note that this can happen, in case he does invite a person who has had a very traditional Eastern upbringing.

While in Malaysia, a foreigner is bound to be invited to many Malaysian meals. Obviously, there will come a time when you (the foreigner) will bite into something that you simply cannot swallow. What do you do with that piece of "offending" food?

If you are eating Chinese food with chopsticks, very often

you will be provided with a side plate where it is expected that bones and other inedible bits of food be placed. I would suggest that you discreetly put the piece that did not agree with you among the other bits and pieces on this side plate. If a side plate is not provided, as in the case where your Chinese host is more Westernised and eats with fork and spoon instead of chopsticks and rice bowl, then you may put the unwanted piece of food on your dinner plate. It would not look in the least odd – go ahead and do so.

Nowadays, if you are eating a Malay or Indian meal, especially in a restaurant, you would normally find you have a side plate, which is there for you to use as you will. However, if it is Northern Indian food you are eating, perhaps the side plate would be used for bread (e.g. naan, paratha, puri). Even so, it is still perfectly acceptable to put the piece of inedible food on the side plate (of course you would move the bread onto your own plate first!) and ask for another side plate. You could also put what you can't swallow on your main plate or banana leaf.

As I've mentioned before, we Asians are not so strict about rules and regulations of eating and I doubt anyone would bat an eyelid if you removed something from your mouth right in the middle of a meal.

There are no hard-and-fast rules about second helpings. If you feel you want to eat some more, your Malaysian host would be more than delighted. We Malaysians are always pleased when foreigners enjoy our food. In fact you will find that your Malaysian host is forever asking you to "help yourself to some more food." or "You must try this dish, it's very special!"

On the other side of the coin, to say "no" needs a little sensitivity on your part. Instead of offending your Malaysian hostess (she might have spent half the night preparing this particular dish for you) you simply take what is offered. If you don't like it or can't eat it, leave it on your plate. To say "no" outright can and very often does offend a Malaysian.

3 MAJOR FESTIVALS

As Malaysia is a multi-racial country, different kinds of festivals are celebrated throughout the year. The more common ones are listed below and only the major festivals are described in greater detail later on in the chapter.

Islamic festivals
* Hari Raya Haji
  This festival marks the successful conclusion of the annual Haj (pilgrimage) to Mecca.
* Hari Raya Puasa
  This festival marks the end of the month of Ramadan.
* Maal Hijrah
  This is the Islamic New Year.
* Maulud Nabi
  This is the birthday of the Prophet Muhammad (S.A.W.). The letters S.A.W. stand for Sallalahu Alaihi Wassalam which is Arabic for "May Allah bless Him and grant Him peace". It is customary for all Muslims to say these words every time the Prophet's name is mentioned.

Buddhist/Taoist/Chinese festivals
* Vesak Day
  This is the birthday of Buddha.
* Chinese New Year
* Chap Goh Meh
  This marks the 15th day of the new moon (after Chinese New Year).
* Ching Ming Festival
  Otherwise known as the Festival of the Tomb. On this day, graves are visited, cleaned, and offerings are made.

- Hungry Ghosts Festival
  It is believed that this day marks the release of the hungry spirits of the other world (in search of food).
- Mooncake Festival
  This began as a celebration to mark a successful rebellion against the Mongol rulers. Mooncakes were used to convey secret messages and the lanterns (which are part of this festival) were used to pass signals.

Hindu festivals
- Deepavali
  Otherwise known as the Festival of Lights.
- Thaipusam
  This is a celebration connected with penance and atonement.
- Ponggol
  This is essentially a harvest festival.

Sikh festivals
- Birthday of Guru Nanak, the religious founder of Sikhism (22 December).
- Sikh New Year (13 April)

Christian festivals
- Christmas (25 December)
- Easter (April)

Except where indicated, dates for these festivals change yearly according to lunar reckonings. Also the Islamic, Chinese and Hindu calendars differ, and are not of the same length as the Gregorian calendar. Details of the Islamic, Chinese, and Hindu calendars are mentioned later in this chapter.

For details of the current list of dates (for any particular year), the foreigner is advised to go to the Malaysia Tourism Promotion Board (M.T.P.B.).

While practically all Malaysians celebrate New Year's Eve/ New Year's Day (1 January is a public holiday in most states), at Hari Raya Puasa, the Muslims also celebrate the end of an exhausting month of fasting (Ramadan); at Chinese New Year, the Chinese celebrate the end of one lunar year and the beginning of the next; at Deepavali, the Hindus celebrate the death of a cruel Hindu tyrant; and at Christmas, the Christians celebrate the birth of Christ.

The Open House

The Open House, as we Malaysians know it, is actually a time and day set aside for a person to invite his relatives, friends and acquaintances to his house to join in with whatever festivities he happens to be celebrating. Invitations to Open Houses are usually by word of mouth from the host himself or you will receive an invitation card inviting you to this event. Whether verbally or by card, the time for the Open House will be stated, e.g. from 6.00p.m. to 9.00 p.m. Please make sure that you show up during this period. As Open Houses are so popular these days, you may find your host not at home should you visit at any other time! Many Open Houses however, are held the whole day through with guests coming and going freely but normally not staying too long.They usually stay just long enough for some refreshments and a chat.

Open Houses can be very large and may even be held in hotels.

If you happen to be invited to an Open House which has an R.S.V.P., treat it as you would treat an invitation to any other lunch or dinner. You reply as soon as possible! Invitations for Hari Raya Puasa Open Houses may be worded as follows:

On: The first day of Hari Raya Puasa
or
On: The third day of Hari Raya Puasa
without the actual date because of the uncertainty as to which day the Hari Raya Puasa will actually be!

The Muslims follow the lunar calendar which determines dates by the actual sighting or non-sighting of the moon. The Chinese, the Indians and the Eurasians hold their Open Houses when they celebrate Chinese New Year, Deepavali and Christmas respectively.

For Open Houses at Istanas (and at the homes of other Malaysian dignitaries), a list of times and dates will usually be published in the daily papers and sometimes announced over the television and radio one or two days before the actual event.

An Istana Open House

Appropriate gifts

For all four occasions (Hari Raya Puasa, Chinese New Year, Deepavali and Christmas) flowers are always welcomed and make a very safe gift.

For Hari Raya Puasa, non-Muslims can give small gifts to Muslim children though this is not really expected. We give our children Hari Raya money on Hari Raya morning but we certainly do not expect our non-Malay friends to do the same. If you wish to do so, especially to children of members of your staff, no offence will be taken.

For Chinese New Year, all non-married Chinese get a "red packet" of money (the Ang Pow) from their married relatives and close friends. Like the Malays, the Chinese also do not expect their non-Chinese friends to dish out Ang Pows but if they did, these Ang Pows would be graciously accepted.

If you decide to send your Chinese friend a bouquet of flowers, your florist could combine this arrangement with a basket of mandarin oranges (a symbol of good luck) which would mean a great deal to most Chinese! As a guest coming to a Chinese New Year Open House, you should always bring at least two mandarin oranges along with you to give to your host. This is part of Chinese tradition, but if you came without the mandarin oranges you would be warmly welcomed just the same.

The Ang Pow (red packet)

The Ang Pow, a little red paper envelope containing money in even numbers or matching denominations e.g. $2.00 or $4.00, is a feature we Malaysians automatically associate with any Chinese occasion being celebrated. Especially during the Chinese New Year, these red packets are distributed by the elders and married members of a family to the unmarried and to the children. These red packets are given as tokens of good fortune.

For those who cannot afford to fill these red packets with big amounts to be given away at Chinese New Year the sum of $1.00 or less is acceptable.

A gift of the red packet is also popular when celebrating a birth or a marriage. This is a most practical gift when you are undecided or do not know what present to buy.

If you feel like bringing a small gift for your hostess when you are invited to an Open House, by all means do so. Only remember that exchanges of gifts between adults for these occasions (apart from Christmas) is not the usual practice, so I would suggest your gift does not embarrass your hostess by its size or its price tag. Something unusual from your own country would be very befitting. Alternatively, a gift for the hostess' children would also be nice.

The Ang Pow (Red Packet)

Appropriate dress

You would dress up befitting the festive atmosphere when invited for an Open House, especially if it is held in the evening. A foreign lady should dress as she would to a cocktail or a not very formal dinner. A foreign gentleman would probably have to wear a lounge suit or a long-sleeved batik shirt.

Long-sleeved batik shirt

Please remember that most Eastern cultures, especially the Chinese, consider black a taboo colour when celebrating a happy event. I firmly believe that we must respect other people's beliefs, therefore I strongly suggest you avoid wearing something completely black when invited to a Chinese New Year Open House. Red is the colour you should think of for this occasion. Apparently red has a special magic which drives away all the "bad luck devils"!

If an Open House invitation reads *bebas* (free), this is not an invitation for you to turn up in your blue jeans, T-shirt, and slippers. Even though you are free to wear whatever you wish, you will find that Malaysians *will* dress up when celebrating a festive occasion.

Hari Raya Puasa

It is the celebration to mark the end of the month of Ramadan.

Ramadan (Puasa)

This is the ninth month of the Islamic calendar. During Ramadan, fasting (abstinence from *all* food and water) is rigidly practised daily from sunrise to sunset. This is also the time when all Believers (Muslims) should abstain from evil thoughts and deeds and should try to lead as pure a life as possible. Ramadan was observed by the Prophet Muhammad (S.A.W.) as a form of self-discipline as well as a way of "cleansing" himself.

The fast ends after one lunar month, with the sighting of the new moon. The sighting of the new moon starts the month of Syawal and usually the first three days are celebrated as the Hari Raya Puasa here in Malaysia.

Hari Raya Puasa celebrations

After an exhausting month of fasting, this is a time for joy and happiness (and lots of eating). During the fasting month, it is traditional for Malay families to renovate or redecorate their homes; new curtains are hung and furniture fabrics are changed. Everyone gets new clothes, which they will all wear on Hari Raya day itself.

Foreigners may be amused to see groups of young people going from house to house (it doesn't matter whether they know the owner or not) hoping for a gift of *duit* Raya (Raya money) and some small Raya cakes and soft drinks. As Malays, we do not turn these children away empty-handed.

Important dates in the Muslim calendar

The Muslim calendar also has twelve months. The names of the months are listed below starting with the first month of the Muslim calendar called Muharam up to the twelfth (or last) month of the Muslim calendar called Zulhijah.

1. Muharam – 1st day of the month, Islamic New Year's Day
2. Safar
3. Rabiulawal – 12th day of the month, the Prophet's (S.A.W.) birthday
4. Rabiulakhir
5. Jamadilawal
6. Jamadilakhir
7. Rejab – 27th day of the month, ascension of the Prophet (S.A.W.)
8. Syaaban
9. Ramadan – fasting month
10. Syawal – 1st/2nd/3rd days of the month, Hari Raya Puasa, very lavishly celebrated in Malaysia.
11. Zulkaedah
12. Zulhijah – 10th day of the month, Hari Raya Haji. This marks the end of the Pilgrimage. It is not as lavishly celebrated in Malaysia as it is in most Arab speaking countries, especially in Saudi Arabia.

Chinese New Year

The Chinese New Year is celebrated by *all* the Chinese, whatever their religion – Ancestor Worship, Buddhism, Taoism or Christianity.

This New Year is simply a celebration that marks the end of one lunar calendar year and greets the beginning of the next, and all Chinese join in the celebration!

As a rule, the Chinese work extremely hard the whole year through. The only time that most Chinese take a short, well-earned break is during the Chinese New Year festivities. Here in Malaysia you will find that some Chinese-Malaysians do not turn up for work for as long as two or three weeks.

On the eve of the Chinese New Year, a reunion dinner is held which all family members must try to attend. This dinner is of utmost importance because it is the one occasion when everybody in the family is reunited – perhaps the only time during the whole year that the whole family can be together. It is customary that married daughters join their husband's family.

Chinese New Year celebrations

So important is this reunion dinner that some businesses will even close on this day so as to ensure that everybody arrives home on time.

On the first day itself, it is the normal practice for young people to visit their elders, e.g. parents, in-laws, and grandparents.

On the third or fourth day, depending on family custom, a special meal called the Yee Sang (raw fish with salad) is served. The Yee Sang consists of several types of finely shredded vegetables colourfully placed in small portions mixed with different condiments and a few flakes of raw fish.

Here in Malaysia, a lot of non-Chinese people are invited to participate in this unusual meal. If you find yourself with an invitation to such an event, you might like to know that everyone who helps to toss all the different ingredients of this Yee Sang meal has the hope of being very successful, or will succeed in a very big way some day!

I suppose one can never be too affluent or too successful, so even if you have wall-to-wall wealth, you are still welcome to toss the Yee Sang around for even more wealth and prosperity!

The Chinese New Year visits can go on until the fifteenth day of the new year. This fifteenth day is called Chap Goh Meh by the Hokkiens (one of the main Chinese dialect groups in Malaysia).

The Chinese year is based on the Chinese lunar calendar and the Chinese Zodiac. There are twelve animal signs in the Chinese Zodiac and each new year is named after one of the twelve signs in a cyclical fashion. For easy reference, sets of dates (according to the Western calendar) are listed to correspond with the twelve signs of the Chinese Zodiac. (Please refer to the table on the pages that follow.)

Signs in the Chinese Zodiac

The Year	**The Animal**
10/2/1948 – 28/1/1949 28/1/1960 – 14/2/1961 15/2/1972 – 02/2/1973 02/2/1984 – 19/2/1985 19/2/1996 – 06/2/1997	*The Rat*
11/2/1937 – 30/1/1938 29/1/1949 – 16/2/1950 15/2/1961 – 04/2/1962 03/2/1973 – 22/1/1974 20/2/1985 – 08/2/1986 07/2/1997 – 27/1/1998	*The Ox*
31/1/1938 – 18/2/1939 17/2/1950 – 05/2/1951 05/2/1962 – 24/1/1963 23/1/1974 – 10/2/1975 09/2/1986 – 28/1/1987 28/1/1998 – 15/2/1999	*The Tiger*
19/2/1939 – 07/2/1940 06/2/1951 – 26/1/1952 25/1/1963 – 12/2/1964 11/2/1975 – 30/1/1976 29/1/1987 – 16/2/1988 16/2/1999 – 04/2/2000	*The Rabbit*
08/2/1940 – 26/1/1941 27/2/1952 – 13/2/1953 13/2/1964 – 01/2/1965 31/1/1976 – 17/2/1977 17/2/1988 – 05/2/1989	*The Dragon*
27/1/1941 – 14/2/1942 14/2/1953 – 02/2/1954 02/2/1965 – 20/1/1966 18/2/1977 – 06/2/1978 06/2/1989 – 26/1/1990	*The Snake*

The Year	The Animal
15/2/1942 – 04/2/1943 03/2/1954 – 23/1/1955 04/1/1966 – 08/2/1967 07/2/1978 – 27/1/1979 27/1/1990 – 14/2/1991	*The Horse*
05/2/1943 – 24/1/1944 24/1/1955 – 11/2/1956 09/2/1967 – 29/1/1968 28/1/1979 – 15/2/1980 15/2/1991 – 03/2/1992	*The Goat*
25/1/1944 – 12/2/1945 12/2/1956 – 30/1/1957 30/1/1968 – 16/2/1969 16/2/1980 – 04/2/1981 04/2/1992 – 22/1/1993	*The Monkey*
13/2/1945 – 01/2/1946 31/1/1957 – 17/2/1958 17/2/1969 – 05/2/1970 05/2/1981 – 24/1/1982 23/1/1993 – 09/2/1994	*The Rooster*
02/2/1946 – 21/1/1947 06/2/1970 – 26/1/1971 25/1/1982 – 12/2/1983 10/2/1994 – 30/1/1995	*The Dog*
22/1/1947 – 09/2/1948 08/2/1959 – 27/1/1960 27/1/1971 – 14/2/1972 13/2/1983 – 01/2/1984 31/1/1995 – 18/2/1996	*The Pig*

Deepavali

There are many legends behind the celebration of Deepavali (the Festival of Lights). One of them is the story of a Hindu tyrant, Naragasuran. He was such an extremely cruel king that his people appealed to Lord Krishna to remove him. Lord Krishna answered by having him (Naragasuran) defeated and fatally wounded in battle. Before his death, Naragasuran repented his cruelty and begged Lord Krishna for forgiveness. He asked for one favour, which Lord Krishna granted: instead of weeping for him, all his people should celebrate his death. This we now know as the celebration of Deepavali.

Deepavali is usually in October. Astrology determines the exact day on which the festival should fall.

Deepavali is largely a day for the whole family and also when their non-Hindu friends come to visit.

In the morning, some Hindus would have an oil bath where oil is rubbed onto the head before the actual bathing.

Deepavali celebrations

After that, prayers are said for the whole family (even for those no longer alive). Prayers are led by the head of the family, e.g. the father.

Everyone wears bright new clothes. Children receive presents. Gifts are distributed to the poor and food offered to beggars.

Thaipusam

The other festival celebrated by Hindus in Malaysia is Thaipusam, which usually falls in January. This festival is connected with answered prayers. A person taking part in the Thaipusam procession (the major feature of Thaipusam) might have recovered from an illness or received a promotion at work. Since his prayers have been answered, he must reciprocate by doing some sort of penance to show his gratitude.

A Kavadi bearer

A devotee prepares himself from three weeks to a month before the actual day. On the morning of the festival he bathes and puts on saffron coloured clothes. He also covers his body in holy ash.

He is now ready to pick up the Kavadi. The Kavadi is an arch with spikes whose points enter the devotee's body. On the arch two small pots are placed containing milk which is used to bathe the statue of Lord Subramaniam.

Because of the chanting and the prayers and the general atmosphere of the crowd, the devotee enters into a trance. After the Kavadi is fitted on, a needle (quite large) is pierced through the devotee's tongue.

After he completes his procession, everything is taken out. If he felt no pain throughout the ceremony his vow of penance has been fulfilled.

In Kuala Lumpur the procession takes place at the Batu Caves, which is actually located in the State of Selangor on the outskirts of Kuala Lumpur.

The Hindu calendar
It is primarily based on the lunar cycle but adds on a few days every three years. This correction or addition is made so that it can coincide with the Western calendar as much as possible.

Christmas

My Eurasian friends tell me they cannot speak for the Eurasians living in our neighbouring countries, but Eurasians in Malaysia celebrate Christmas very much the same way other Christians the world over celebrate it, with the exception of one thing: in place of the traditional Christmas lunch, they now hold a Christmas Day Open House. The Open House would usually start at 10.00 a.m. and can go on for as many hours as the host pleases. Food served would be a combination of traditional Christmas "goodies" as well as a range of typical Eurasian cuisine.

Christmas festivities start on Christmas Eve. The whole family is expected to attend Midnight Mass. After this, everyone goes back to the family home (or to the house of the oldest sibling) and has supper there. This meal is very important and everybody ought to try to come. After the meal is over, the exchange of Christmas gifts begin. Even the children get their presents at this time. For this occasion they are allowed to stay up!

Nobody has very much sleep on Christmas Eve! The next morning, everybody gets up early to prepare for the Open House. A Christmas Open House is not restricted to family members – everyone is welcomed – but on the first day, it is normal practice to spend it with one's family. On the second day, visits to friends begin and Christmas gifts are exchanged. Christmas Open Houses can go on for approximately a week. Some even combine their Christmas Open House with their New Year Open House.

4 BIRTHS, BIRTHDAYS, MARRIAGES AND FUNERALS

Malay Customs

Birth
Confinement

As soon as a baby is born, both mother and child have to undergo a period of confinement (*dalam hari*) of forty-four days. During this time neither one of them is allowed to leave the house. This is also the time when the new mother undergoes a rather exhausting programme where she is put on a special diet and is massaged daily so as to restore her to the physical state she enjoyed before the vigorous experience of childbirth.

On the forty-fourth day, the confinement ends (*habis hari*). Some Malay families celebrate this event, others do not; they simply announce that "So-and-so *sudah habis hari*" (So-and-so is no longer in confinement). A token of thanks is usually sent to the mosque.

If the mother has a job, she usually goes back any time after this and life for the mother continues as before. The child starts on his new life now without the restrictions of confinement.

When to visit

Guests are welcome to visit the new arrival anytime during the confinement period (either at the hospital or at home). If you are visiting at home, do not do so too early in the morning because this is when the midwife cleans the baby and "looks after" the mother. Visits also should be short as it is not advisable for the new mother to sit up too long at any one time. Some families do not allow the new mother to leave her bedroom. If a guest comes to visit, she may be asked to go into the new mother's bedroom to see her.

Appropriate gifts

There are no hard-and-fast rules regarding gifts; everything is always accepted graciously. While the mother is still in the hospital, flowers are always popular. Gifts when visiting at home are usually for the child.

If you know for a fact that the new parents could do with some financial help, a gift of cash is always welcomed. But, when giving money, do this discreetly. You could put the money into an envelope, hand it to the new mother with such words as "Something small towards the child's savings".

Ceremonies to mark the birth

There are many, many ceremonies before and after the birth. Every family of course can decide which ceremonies they want to observe and which they want to do away with.

If you are not a Muslim, it is very likely that you will not be invited to any of these many ceremonies as they tend to be religious in nature. Even if the ceremony happens to be a traditional one (rather than religious), it would be accompanied by prayers.

As a non-Muslim invited to such an event, you would be invited simply as an observer – which can be quite awkward at times because all the other guests (Muslims) may be asked to participate during the ceremony.

Some ceremonies which you may be invited to are:

Naik Buaian – this is when the child is officially introduced to his cradle.

Potong Jambul – this is when the child's head is shaven to "cleanse" him for his life outside the mother's womb. This shaving was a command given by the Prophet Muhammad (S.A.W.) on all newborn babies.

Jejak Tanah   – this is when the child's feet are introduced to the feel of the earth for the first time. He can now leave the house and take in fresh air without the fear of being harmed by evil spirits.

Appropriate dress

Since there is a certain element of religion present in any ceremony, I would suggest that a female guest wear something that covers the arms and legs. A Muslim lady should also come with something with which to cover the head.

As most ceremonies are conducted with the guests sitting on the floor, turning up in a tight skirt can be both awkward and embarrassing. For a male guest, a long-sleeved batik shirt is always safe.

Birthday
Celebrations/Ceremonies

For those who are more exposed to Western influences (not necessarily the younger generation), birthdays are celebrated much the same as in the West, i.e. with birthday cards and gifts, a birthday cake and candles, a birthday party, and a birthday song.

However, with the more traditional (not necessarily the older generation), birthdays are celebrated more as a token of thanks, or gratitude, towards Allah for His gift of longevity and general good health. For this type of birthday celebration, prayers are usually held (*kenduri*) where some sort of token, usually food, is given to the local mosque and/or to the less fortunate. Some of us celebrate both ways.

Landmark birthdays normally start at the age of 60 (especially for a man, who is proud to reach this age in good health). After that, birthdays are probably celebrated (or observed) on a grand scale every five years. After the 80th year most Malay men celebrate each year following, as they want no regrets to be felt should they not be able to reach the next birthday.

Appropriate gifts

No taboos whatsoever here. Flowers are always appropriate (for both sexes). If cash is given, this is usually enclosed in a birthday card which you would hand to the birthday person saying something like: "Your gift is in here as well", pointing to the envelope.

Appropriate dress

If you, as a foreigner, are invited to a birthday party which is being given in the Western way, anything festive would be acceptable. Besides, most birthday invitations would state a dress code, therefore you would dress accordingly. I have seen many birthday girls (of all generations) wearing black to celebrate the occasion. I suppose this means that there are no taboos if the colour black is being worn by the guests as well.

Though it is not likely that a non-Muslim will be invited to the more traditional birthday celebration (because of its religious nature), some Malays do invite non-Muslims to this event after the prayers have been said, e.g. a Muslim guest would probably be invited for Maghrib (early evening) prayers and non-Muslims would be asked to come at dinner time. Even though non-Muslim guests may have missed the prayers, I would still advise the ladies (this is not so important to the man as he is not likely to turn up in shorts) to turn up in something appropriate, i.e. a dress that is not too short and/ or not too tight because it must be remembered that the Malay ladies who did participate in the prayers would still be present when the other guests arrive.

To dress too provocatively would show a certain amount of disrespect to these Malay ladies! For the foreign gentleman, unless a dress code is stated, your long-sleeved batik shirt is what you should wear.

Marriage
The different ceremonies

There are many ceremonies leading up to the actual wedding itself. A foreigner is most likely to be invited to the final ceremony – the Bersanding (sitting-in-state) – in the solemnization of a Malay wedding. This is a most colourful event where the bridal couple is treated as Royalty-for-the-Day (Raja Sehari) and relatives and friends come to wish them well. If you happen to be close to the bride or the groom (or both) you may be invited to a few ceremonies preceding the Bersanding ceremony. These could be:

The Hantar Tanda – the statement of intent from the groom's side.

The Bertunang – The engagement

The Akad Nikah – The actual marriage ceremony

The Berinai – The ceremony where henna is painted on the bride and groom's palms and fingertips.

Of all the above, the Akad Nikah is the one compulsory ceremony as this is when the couple are religiously and legally declared husband and wife.

The Bersanding ceremony

The bridal couple sit on a raised dais (*pelamin*). Behind the bride's chair stands her attendant and behind the groom's chair stands his. These two people have the duty of attending to the bride and groom while they sit in state.

As soon as the bride and groom are seated on the dais, the Blessing Ceremony begins.

If you are a foreigner having to do this honour for the first time, a woman relative seated at the edge of the dais will coach you as to what should be done.

The normal procedure is as follows: take a small handful of scented leaves and scented flower petals (*bunga rampai*) and scatter them onto the open palm of the bride and groom. Always begin with the groom's right palm and end with the bride's left palm (Follow this procedure throughout). Next, take the small bouquet of leaves and dip in the paste-like liquid. Shake a few drops onto the open palm of the bride and groom (*menepung tawar*). Then you will be asked to scatter a few grains of saffron rice over the shoulders of the bride and groom and/or sprinkle a few drops of scented water on the open palm of the bride and groom. Once you have completed the above, you step down from the dais. Usually at this point, you will be handed a gilded hard-boiled egg encased in a golden or silver holder (*bunga telur*). Eggs symbolise fertility.

All guests go home with a *bunga telur*, although these days it may not consist of a hard-boiled egg. Alternatives can be sweets or chocolates shaped like eggs.

Appropriate gifts
Unlike in England where guests may be given a list of suggested presents and the store where they can be bought, in Malaysia a guest can make up his own mind as to what he feels is the most appropriate.

The Bersanding

Anything towards the couple's new home would always be welcomed (especially practical gifts like toasters and rice-cookers). If you happen to know that the couple could do with a little extra cash, by all means give them a gift of money. If you opt for this, do so discreetly by handing it to a parent of the bride when you arrive or just before you leave. You would put the money in a small envelope (or a small packet) and quietly press it into the palm of this parent when you shake his/her hand in greeting or farewell. You would also lean forward to whisper: "A small gift for the young couple – to help them out with their new home" or words to that effect. Wedding presents can either be sent in advance (usually to the bride's parent's house) or brought with you.

Appropriate dress

The Malays would all probably turn up in the National Dress (both men and women). If you have been looking for the opportunity to wear your Baju Melayu, here is the perfect time to do so. Believe me, the family of the bridal couple will be absolutely delighted!

Otherwise, a male guest is normally expected to turn up in a lounge suit (in a hotel or restaurant) or a long-sleeved batik shirt (at home).

A female guest can dress up to her heart's content. I would, however, suggest something that covers the knees or even the ankles. If invited to the house, a non-Malay guest may find herself invited to sit on the floor along with the Malay ladies. Having to struggle to sit and to stand up again just won't do (not to mention trying *not* to show too much leg)! Dressy trouser suits would be the answer here. By and large, trousers (if worn modestly and elegantly) are an accepted mode of dress in Malay company.

Funeral

When to call/pay last respects

The time between death and burial is minimal. If you want to pay your last respects before the body is buried, do so as soon as you are told of the death.

For a short period of time the body of the deceased is placed in the centre of the living room or the hall to give everyone a chance to offer prayers and have a last look before the burial ceremony.

As a non-Muslim, you may or may not be invited to witness the body at close range. If you are not, it is best that you sit outside and try to inform a member of the family that you are there to express your condolences. Although you may not have a chance to see the bereaved, they will no doubt be informed that you took the trouble to come. Leaving your calling card behind is permitted.

The normal mourning period is 100 days. For the first three nights following the death, prayers at home are held daily. After that, the next prayers are held on the seventh day, followed by the fortieth day and, finally, on the hundredth day.

It is highly unlikely for a non-Muslim to be invited to any of these prayers. Therefore, it is advisable that you do not visit at these times.

If you did not visit the bereaved before the burial, you can do so during the mourning period. Try not to visit in the early evening (Maghrib) as prayers are held during this time. Maghrib in Malaysia usually starts sometime between 7.15 and 7.30 p.m.

Sending of wreaths and condolence letters

One does not normally send wreaths to a Malay funeral, although they will not be thrown away if received. What usually happens is that the wreath will be disassembled and the flowers used to sprinkle over the new grave.

Although sending a letter of condolence is not a Malay practice, when received it is always appreciated. Perhaps a non-Muslim would be well advised to send a condolence letter or a condolence card since you may find it difficult and inappropriate to do anything else.

A cash donation can be given to the family of the deceased if you feel they need it. Sometimes a small box or bowl is strategically placed so that you can drop your donation into it. Otherwise, pass your donation (in an envelope) to a responsible member of the family, politely stating that you hope the family might be able to use it for the funeral or the many ceremonies (*kenduri*) held afterwards. *Kenduri* to mark a death is usually attended by family and close family friends only.

Appropriate dress

The Malay will normally turn up in the Baju Melayu (both men and women) using the colour white (or predominantly white). The ladies will cover their heads with a *selendang* (shawl). As all ceremonies dealing with death are religious, make sure that you respect this and turn up in something sober.

For a non-Muslim lady, arms and knees must be covered. Your dress should not be bright with loud prints or floral designs. Dark colours like grey, blue, and brown are advisable. Wearing a hat is optional. Trousers in dark colours are also appropriate.

For a non-Muslim gentleman, a dark lounge suit, a dark tie, and a plain shirt are the appropriate attire. Some may feel it too hot to wear a jacket and it is not always necessary for them to wear one as long as the tie and trousers are dark and the shirt is plain.

Chinese Customs

Birth
Confinement

The usual confinement period for both mother and child is one full month following the birth of the child. Within this time, neither one is allowed out of the house. The mother is advised to rest in bed and not to walk about too much for the first two weeks after the delivery.

Normally, a close family member, a relative, or an employed *pui-yit* (a kind of midwife employed specially during the confinement period) is given the task of looking after the newborn and his mother right up to the baby's "Full Moon".

It should be noted here that in the context of birth, the Chinese words for Full Moon actually mean "Full Month". This month refers to the newborn's first 30 days starting from birth. However, the word for month also means moon in Chinese. The Chinese in Malaysia have used the term Full Moon instead of Full Month to refer to the first 30 days of an infant's life. This common though inaccurate use of the term Full Moon is adopted in this book as it is common usage that is significant.

During the confinement, the mother is also put under a strict diet of healthy, "heaty", strength-restoring foods. The more conservative ones will still abstain from eating certain foods until the hundredth day after the delivery.

After the month is over, the mother undergoes various purifications and the family celebrates the baby's Full Moon. A feast is held on this day. Whether it is on a small or grand scale depends on the family. By tradition the baby's head is shaved, although more modern mothers do not find this necessary and may not observe this.

Soon after the Full Moon, the baby begins to lead the normal day-to-day existence of any baby and the mother is allowed to resume the lifestyle she followed before the birth.

When to visit

Though I am told by my Chinese-Malaysian friends that they no longer strictly observe the time limit forbidding friends to visit, traditionally, visitors are not allowed to see the new mother and child until the child has completed his Full Moon. Being a foreigner and not fully aware of whether or not the family you plan to visit observes traditional Chinese customs and values, I would suggest you ring first to enquire as to when it would be appropriate for you to visit.

Personally, I have visited many Chinese-Malaysian friends as soon as I hear of the birth, i.e. at the hospital itself.

Appropriate gifts

When still in hospital or during the confinement period, popular gifts for the mother are: flowers, brandy or Dom Benedictine (or any tonic liquor), Chinese herbs, essence of chicken (prepacked) and for the baby, usual gifts are toys and baby clothes.

Flowers are more appropriate if delivered to the hospital than to the house. However, there is no harm in sending the flowers to the house if you cannot personally visit the mother and her newborn.

The one safe gift is always the Ang Pow (red packet – please see detailed explanation on page 34) especially if you are undecided as to what you should buy.

The amount enclosed in the Ang Pow is up to you.

If it is money that you have decided to give, please remember to put it in the standard red Ang Pow envelope. If you do not have one available, a small red or pink envelope is also acceptable. These envelopes are readily available at most stationery shops. A white envelope should never be used other than at a death!

Ceremonies to mark the birth

While there may be several ceremonies before and after the birth, here in Malaysia, Chinese-Malaysians mainly observe two ceremonies.

On the third day following the birth – close relatives come to the house to celebrate this event.

The Full Moon – I am told that this is when the child is given a name (sometimes on an experimental basis). If the child turns sickly and weak, the name will be changed and may be changed time and time again until a suitable name is found. Thus, many Chinese-Malaysians have aliases on their identity cards.

The Full Moon ceremony is not confined only to family members and you may very well be invited to this, should the parents of the newborn be close friends of yours.

A present of some sort would be appropriate. Apart from the usual baby gifts like clothes, toys, prams, etc., the Ang Pow (red packet) is a popular choice, especially if this celebration is held in a restaurant. Lugging along a big gift would be most cumbersome!

Jewellery (especially gold trinkets like anklets, bracelets and gold bars) is a popular gift for the baby between family members and close relatives.

Appropriate dress
Though religion may not come into the picture, tradition might. The Chinese tend to frown on black being worn during happy occasions. Please bear this in mind! Bright colours would be your best bet.

Birthday
Celebrations/Ceremonies
For those exposed to Western ways, a birthday is often celebrated the way their Western counterparts would, i.e. a party in a brightly decorated room (or house), presents from friends, and the blowing of the birthday candles on a specially made birthday cake. Everyone joins in to sing "Happy Birthday".

Traditional birthdays are often celebrated on a grand scale, especially the 60th birthday. The children are expected to plan and organise such an event. Relatives and friends, whether Chinese or non-Chinese, are invited to join in with the family to celebrate such a happy occasion. Some celebrations are held at home,although many families hold such grand parties in restaurants.

Appropriate gifts
Certain Chinese families are a little superstitious about birthday gifts. A few are considered taboo. I suggest you consult a Chinese friend if you are not too sure whether the present you have picked out is acceptable or not.

Flowers are not an appropriate birthday gift as flowers are associated with death to most Chinese. Please also do not give clocks or watches either, especially to the older generation as clocks mean "time's up" to the more superstitious Chinese. For a successful businessman, a scroll with a meaningful Chinese proverb written on it is always appropriate.

Appropriate dress
Anything bright or colourful. If you are wearing sombre or dark colours, do wear gold or bright jewellery. This is one of the best occasions for a guest to dress up (besides wedding celebrations).

If you are provided with a birthday invitation, an appropriate dress code is bound to be included. Otherwise, a female guest is best seen in red (or any bright colour) and a male guest in a long-sleeved batik shirt.

Marriage
The different ceremonies
Traditionally, a marriage is arranged between the two families and not between the boy and girl in question. Nowadays this may not be the case for every Chinese couple but parents and older relatives still have quite a lot of say in this matter, especially if the young couple still live with their respective parents.

Although there is no ceremony held to "match-up" the couple's horoscopes, this event is considered extremely important and most Chinese families will insist on it.

If everything turns out in their favour, the astrologer is called again to fix a good time (and sometimes an appropriate place) for the wedding.

The three ceremonies that most Chinese in Malaysia observe are:

Civil Marriage	– this is when the young couple are registered (legally) as husband and wife.
Tea Ceremony	– this is an old Chinese custom where the newlyweds offer tea to the elders (especially their new in-laws).

These two ceremonies are usually attended by family and *very* close friends only.

Reception/Dinner – this is when everybody celebrates. Relatives, friends and acquaintances are all invited.

The Wedding Reception/Dinner

As a foreigner, it is likely that you will be invited to this event. Nowadays, receptions and dinners are usually held at restaurants and hotels. If it is a dinner you are invited to, a full course Chinese meal is served, which is definitely a chopstick affair. It is best you know how to handle a pair (please refer to the section on "Table Manners" on page 24).

Throughout the dinner, the newlyweds and their parents go from table to table to invite their guests to join them in the traditional "Yum Seng" (bottoms up). For those not in the know, do check the bridegroom's drink before you Yum Seng merrily with him. It is most likely that you will end up tipsy (and not the groom) as he could be drinking only Chinese tea instead of brandy!

Foreigners will be amazed to see the bride probably changing her gown at least two or three times during the wedding dinner. She would probably enter wearing the traditional Western wedding gown in white. She might then change into a modern cheongsam or a traditional Chinese wedding costume and finally emerge in a Western-style evening gown. At the end of the dinner, the newlyweds and their parents will be at the door to thank all their guests for coming.

Appropriate gifts
The Chinese are usually very superstitious. It is best to check beforehand that the present you want to give is not in any way seen as taboo or that it holds any negative connotations. The Ang Pow (the red packet) is an acceptable gift. Gifts of shoes, handkerchiefs and clocks are not recommended. I am reminded time and time again that a clock is especially frowned on because it is associated with "Time's up, death's knell calls". Gifts for the house or anything ornamental or even something from your own country will all be accepted graciously.

The best time for you to send your present is a day or two before the wedding date. You would usually send it to the house where the bridal room has been set up. This procedure may vary from couple to couple so it might be best that you first check with the bride or bridegroom.

Appropriate dress
As for all weddings, guests should dress extra carefully and look extra festive. If a dress code is not included in the invitation, a wise choice for a gentleman is either a lounge suit (in a hotel or restaurant) or a long-sleeved batik shirt (at home). For a lady, I must stress again that black is considered taboo on happy occasions. If a wedding is not a happy occasion, I don't know what is!

Funeral
When to call/pay last respects
In China the coffin is often kept in the house for several weeks. Due to the climate in Malaysia, the coffin is usually

kept between three days to one week either at home or at the funeral parlour. If you decide to pay your last respects before the burial, you can do so.

You may be given some lighted joss-sticks to hold for praying. If you feel you ought not to take part because of your religious convictions, politely decline the offered joss-sticks, stating your own religion. The bereaved family and the attending monks (if it is a traditional Buddhist or Taoist funeral ceremony) will understand and not take offence. Food and drinks are provided for those who come to call.

If you are an extremely close friend of the family of the deceased, you may be invited to take part in the funeral procession. The funeral procession is usually lined up as follows:

- The numerous banner-holders. Each banner will proclaim virtues of the deceased. These banners are usually led by a pair of large white lanterns on poles on which the family name and the age of the deceased are written out in blue ink or paint.
- The musicians. They make all sorts of loud noises to drive the evil spirits away.
- The hearse itself which contains the coffin, wreaths, and all the paper images which will be burnt at the grave. These paper images are replicas of things the deceased might need in the next world.
- Closest kin and relatives.
- Other mourners and friends.

As a mark of respect, the funeral procession normally starts on foot. After a short distance, everyone will get into their cars or hired buses (for mourners not driving) to proceed to the cemetery.

Mourning can be very long. Nowadays, this is usually one hundred days, though the more traditional families will go on for up to two and a half years.

During the mourning period, it is the custom for the family of the deceased to wear a label pinned onto a sleeve to indicate they are in mourning. It is the usual practice now, however, to simply wear sombre coloured clothes.

If you missed the funeral, a memorial service may also be held which you might be able to attend. It is best to check with a member of the family concerned whether your attendance would be acceptable to the family or not.

Sending of wreaths/condolence letters

Wreaths are always present at a Chinese funeral. By all means send one if you feel you should. Sometimes donations can be given either to the family or to the favourite charity of the deceased. If the second is the case, you will find boxes on tables stating where your donation will go.

Donations should always be sent to the place where the deceased is lying. Please put your contribution in a white envelope. All donations are to be delivered before the burial day (on the day itself is still all right) as it is considered not right to accept donations after the burial.

Sweets and red thread are distributed to those who have come. Please remember that these items should be accepted as they are believed to protect you from the spirits. To refuse would offend the bereaved family especially if they are very traditional.

Appropriate dress

Although the family and relatives of the deceased will be dressed in mourning colours of black, white, grey, dark blue, and pale green (depending on how closely related they are to the deceased), anyone attending a Chinese funeral should also turn up in something equally sombre. Please do not wear purple. Safe colours are grey, blue, and white. The ladies may or may not want to wear a hat. Trousers can be worn.

A gentleman ought to wear a dark lounge suit (with a dark tie and a plain shirt) or, if it is too warm, a dark pair of trousers with a dark tie and a plain shirt.

Indian Customs

Birth

Confinement

This usually lasts between a month to forty-one days after a birth. Before a child is given a name (usually on the sixteenth day) he and his mother are considered ceremonially unclean. However, on this special occasion, the child is given a name and, for the first time since the birth, he is dressed up in fancy clothes and jewellery. After this, the child is considered purified although he and his mother continue to be in confinement.

At the end of the thirty or forty-one days, both child and mother begin their lives as normal. The mother can go back to work and the child is now free from the restrictions of the confinement period. However, the first place the mother and child should visit outside the home is the temple.

When to visit

Non-Indian friends are welcome to visit mother and child either at the hospital or at home. A visit at home might be a little more convenient because of the absence of rigid hospital rules. If you decide to visit the new arrival during the confinement period, chances are you'll find the baby and the mother at home as leaving the house (for both mother and child) is discouraged during this time.

Appropriate gifts

All gifts are accepted with thanks. There are no restrictions here. No present is looked upon as taboo or bad luck.

A gift of cash to a member of your staff is completely acceptable, although to your own peers' children this is not so usual. A small piece of jewellery (a small bangle/earrings) to children of close friends is also a popular gift.

At the hospital, a bouquet of flowers for the new mother would be appropriate.

Ceremonies to mark the birth

Even before a child is conceived, some Indian families make sure that the would-be parents undergo certain purification rites.

The first of such purification rites is done on the fourth day of the marriage.

The second, performed a little later, is to pray for the birth of a son. Sons are always hoped for as only sons can perform certain rites during the father's funeral.

Daughters can prove to be expensive as they have to be provided with dowries! By tradition (although the more modern Indian families have done away with this) a female has to provide a male (the bridegroom) with a dowry. The more eligible the young man (in terms of profession and affluence), the more impressive the dowry!

The Seemantham

Usually, as the mother enters her seventh month of pregnancy, a ceremony is held at her marital home where her parents prepare to take her back to their home to await the birth of her child in her own (family) home.

If you happen to be invited to this ceremony, it is customary to bring a gift for the expectant mother. Those who know will come with colourful glass bangles which they would slip onto the young woman's wrist.

Don't worry, if you came without these colourful glass bangles, they will be given to you. The family will make sure there are enough bangles for all their guests.

The Sixteenth Day Ceremony

A name-giving ceremony is usually held on the sixteenth day after the child's birth. All dressed up and purified, this is the occasion the parents can show off their new bundle of joy!

The more traditional families will name a son after a Hindu god and a daughter after a Hindu goddess, although I am told that this is *not* compulsory!

If you are a close friend of the family, you may be invited to witness this Sixteenth Day ceremony and join in the celebration.

Appropriate dress

Birth being a generally joyous occasion, you will find that the family of the baby will make the effort to dress up in beautiful clothes which are brightly coloured.

Although there are no restrictions as to what a guest can or cannot wear, it might be worth noting that some part of the ceremony may take place on the floor, as most Eastern ceremonies do! To be wriggling in a short dress would be most inappropriate, especially when you see the other ladies sitting so gracefully with their saris elegantly covering all the parts of their body that should be covered!

Bear in mind that a dress which easily covers your legs would be appropriate here or you may want to opt for a loose but elegant pair of trousers. Even though you are not prohibited from wearing any particular colour, black may not be quite appropriate as this is a celebration and Easterners tend to dress up in bright, happy colours when celebrating. If anything, black is considered taboo because of its association with sombre events, e.g. a funeral, but if it happens to be your favourite colour, I have been assured that you won't be frowned upon.

Birthday
Celebrations/Ceremonies

Though Indians are rather conservative in upbringing, Western influences are, nevertheless, evident in certain areas. The more modern Indians would probably observe their birthday in the Western way and a foreigner attending such a birthday would then witness the sort of birthday atmosphere evident at most birthday parties celebrated throughout the Western world. There would be a birthday cake, lots of birthday presents, the room would be colourfully decorated.

However, no matter how modern or how westernised an Indian is, his traditional birthday (determined by the Hindu calendar unless he is an Indian-Muslim) is observed almost without exception. For this there is no party held, only prayers. Even though this traditional ceremony may be sober and serious in nature, foreigners may attend.

A landmark age for the Indian gentleman is his 60th birthday. For this special occasion, a celebration is held to pray for his continued longevity and good health. His wife is included as part of this birthday ceremony because, as at their wedding, the Mangal Sutra (Thali) is once again fastened around her neck (see p 69). All expenditure for this 60th birthday celebration must be borne by the children.

It is interesting to observe that the more traditional Indian widow will cease to celebrate her birthday after the death of her husband. This is because Hindu custom dictates that as soon as a lady becomes a widow, she can no longer participate in any joyous occasion. My Indian friends, however, add that this custom is not so rigidly adhered to nowadays.

Appropriate gifts

Whether you bring a birthday gift or not is left entirely up to you. There are absolutely no taboo gifts, including the gift of money. Cash is not given openly. Please enclose it in an envelope or inside a birthday card. Indicate that your envelope or birthday card holds your present inside. You would normally do this by saying something like "It isn't very much but I thought you could choose something you like on your own."

Appropriate dress

My Indian friends are forever reminding me that Indians love to dress in bright colours for festive occasions! As a foreigner I would suggest that you follow their example as closely as you can and try not to turn up in dull colours.

Birthday invitation cards very often state a dress code.

If it doesn't, the most appropriate dress for a man would be a long-sleeved batik shirt. For a lady something cheerful and not too short would be the most appropriate.

Marriage
The different ceremonies

If a marriage is arranged by the two families, a priest (from each side) is called to compare the prospective bride's and bridegroom's horoscopes. If all is well, then the marriage is agreed upon. Once a match has been decided on, the very important question of the dowry is brought up and settled. After that, an engagement (betrothal) ceremony is held. At this ceremony, the marriage contract is drawn up. Once both sides agree, this contract should not be broken.

It is interesting to note that a marriage proposal among the Hindus usually comes from the girl's side, as they are the ones that have to provide the dowry. Although traditional families still abide by this, in modern practice, the proposal can and does come from the boy's side, especially here in Malaysia.

Sharing of expenses is also becoming a common practice, e.g. the boy's side pays for the actual wedding ceremony and the girl's side pays for the engagement ceremony.

It is unlikely that guests will be invited to the dowry ceremony as this is something that is usually witnessed by the two families only. However, for the engagement (betrothal) party, close friends are invited regardless of whether they are Indians or not.

The wedding ceremony

This is very similar to the Malay Bersanding Ceremony. The marriage ceremony is usually held in the bride's house. At a pre-arranged time, the bridegroom and his entourage will arrive. The bride and bridegroom will sit side by side on a decorated dais. They may have to repeat verses recited by the priest present.

As the wedding ceremony begins, prayers are offered to the god Ganesh (the god with the elephant face). During this offering, a coconut is broken in half with a sharp *parang* (chopper or cleaver) by the priest. This priest tries his best to halve the coconut as neatly as possible. A neatly halved coconut signifies a good marriage (i.e. this is a good omen).

A coconut is used because it is pure, with the water inside untouched. This ceremony is also used as a symbol of prosperity and fertility.

The bridegroom is then expected to tie a saffron string around the bride's neck. A gold pendant, called the Mangal Sutra, is attached to the saffron string.

After this is completed, the bride and bridegroom will step down from the dais and will take seven steps around a sacred fire lit in the centre of the marriage room or hall. This action signifies that the couple are now religiously married. Non-Hindu guests are allowed to witness this unique ceremony.

Appropriate gifts

You won't find a list of suggested gifts when you receive your invitation card! A wedding present is left totally up to the discretion of the guest. There are no restrictions as to the sort of gift one can give, including the gift of cash. If it is cash you have decided on, this is not given uncovered. You would either enclose it in an envelope or slip it in your wedding card. This can be handed to the newlyweds or someone close to them (their parents).

Should you decide to buy a present, bringing it with you to the reception or sending it in advance to the bride's or bridegroom's parents' house are both acceptable.

Appropriate dress

The Indian guests (especially the ladies) are very likely to turn up in their most stunning costumes. They would most probably expect you to turn up in equally attractive attire! The usual guide for a gentleman is the lounge suit (hotel and restaurant) or a long-sleeved batik shirt (at home). A lady can wear what she would normally wear for any other sort of wedding. If you feel that gloves and a hat are appropriate, by all means put them on!

Funeral
When to call/pay last respects
After a death, there is adequate time for you to pay your last respects before the body is taken away to be cremated. Non-Hindus can call at the home of the deceased where the body is placed for this purpose.

The bodies of Hindus are cremated. In the past, widows were supposed to be burnt alive, along with their dead husbands. This practice was observed until 1926 when the Suttee (as it is called) was prohibited by law by the Government of India.

If you should decide to go to the funeral, it might be worth your while to note that the ladies will *not* go to the crematorium – even if it is her husband that has just died! The ladies remain at home while the men go to perform the last rites.

Also, during the funeral ceremony at home, the widow will take off her Mangal Sutra (the gold pendant attached to a saffron string which she was given during her wedding ceremony) and she is not supposed to wear it again.

The mourning period is anything between a month and forty-one days, during which time you are permitted to visit the family of the deceased.

From the moment a person dies, the normal prayers which are usually performed in the house are stopped until the sixteenth day. The family does not even go to the temple until then. On this special morning, the house is washed and cleaned.

The men of the family take a boat out to the open seas to perform special purification rites to mark this event. The ladies must make sure that the house is "cleansed" before they return. When the men come back, they bathe themselves to complete this purification. A priest is called to bless the house. The house is now no longer considered taboo (which is usually the Eastern attitude whenever something is connected with death).

If the deceased was a close friend of yours, you may be invited to witness this sixteenth day event. For this, you would wear the usual clothes befitting a sombre occasion— Nothing too loud or ostentatious.

Widows no longer wear the decorative spot on their forehead. This decorative spot can be worn by single girls if they wish to. After marriage, it is a custom for married ladies to do so. Widows, however, are not supposed to wear it.

Sending of wreaths/condolence letters

If you want to send a wreath, make sure you send it before the body leaves for the crematorium. All wreaths accompany the body when it leaves the house.

A condolence letter is always appropriate and very much appreciated. If you feel the family of the deceased might benefit from a small cash donation from you, by all means give it to them. The money can be enclosed in an envelope and handed to the bereaved or any close family member. Do add, politely, that you hope your "envelope" will be useful to the family. They will understand and appreciate your action.

Appropriate dress

The family of the deceased will wear white or light-coloured clothes for the funeral.

A foreign lady should turn up in subdued colours such as grey, blue or brown. Whether you feel you should wear a hat is up to you. A foreign gentleman should wear a dark lounge suit with a dark tie and a plain shirt or, if it is too warm, a pair of dark trousers teamed with a plain shirt and a dark tie.

5 CORRECT FORMS OF ADDRESS

When Independence was declared in 1957, nine Malay rulers from nine different states still existed. Now that there was officially one country, what would happen to these rulers? A solution was found where one ruler would be voted in among the nine to become the Supreme Head for a period of five years until all nine rulers had been elected. Voting (until today) is only allowed among the rulers themselves. Election into this office is usually determined by state seniority, that is, how long a ruler has been on his *state* throne; the longer the reign, the more senior the ruler.

Thus, the office of the Yang DiPertuan Agong (He Who is Made Supreme Lord) was created, with the first Agong being the ruler of Negeri Sembilan. The present Yang DiPertuan Agong is from the state of Perak, last of the nine states to be elected into this office.

As a result of the complicated and often ruthless political manoeuvres of the past, today four states, namely Melaka, Penang, Sabah and Sarawak are under appointed governors. While he is in office, a governor takes on the role and the responsibility of a Head-of-State. The capital city of Malaysia is Kuala Lumpur. It is known as the Federal Territory. The Yang DiPertuan Agong as King of the whole of Malaysia resides in Kuala Lumpur as does the Prime Minister as head of the Federal Government.

It can be seen that the social and political hierarchy is very complex in Malaysia. Therefore the need to know the proper forms of address must never be underestimated. At every step (or level) of the ladder, there is an appropriate or correct form of address.

There are the Heads-of-State (the Yang DiPertuan Agong,

the Sultans, Raja, Yang DiPertuan Besar, and the Governors), the senior members of the Federal Government (headed by the Prime Minister) and the individual State Governments (each headed by a Chief Minister), people like the Cabinet Ministers, Senators, Parliamentary Secretaries, and other Members of Parliament.

The Civil Service includes members of the Administrative and Diplomatic Service, the Defence Force (i.e. the Army, Navy, and Air Force), the Police, the Judicial and Legal Service. Various academic institutions and statutory bodies are also under the Civil Service.

To take care of religious matters, there are the religious officers of various ranks in the Muslim, Christian, Buddhist, and Hindu faiths.

There is an appropriate form of address for everyone with a position or designation in the various organisations mentioned above; a form of address which he acquired either by virtue of his office or by his own title (or a combination of both). Whatever the reasons, the majority expect to be addressed in the appropriate manner.

Since there are titles and positions galore in Malaysia, it would be almost impossible not to meet up with someone who has to be correctly addressed at any type of function one happens to attend.

Functions can be categorised very broadly as official and non-official (private). There is also the social function (e.g. births, birthdays, marriages, and other important events) which can either be official (e.g. the birthday of a Head-of-State) or private. Funerals whether official or not are also occasions where people meet each other.

Official functions include:
- Royal functions – these are either functions which are hosted by a Royal Head-of-State (in his official capacity) or functions where a Royal Head-of-State is invited (again, in his official capacity).

- Government functions – these are functions given by the Government and can be hosted by any government representative either from the political sector or the Civil Service (e.g. a Minister or a Permanent Secretary).
- Diplomatic functions – these are functions given by the Diplomatic Corps (e.g. National Day, Monarch's Birthday, and other important anniversaries or events).

Private functions, whether given by the King, a Minister, or anybody else for that matter, are considered private as long as they are hosted in a private capacity.

Meeting a V.I.P. even in a private capacity is not an automatic invitation to address him simply by his first name. A tremendous amount of common sense and discretion has to be used in such situations. My one word of advice: if you have to err, err on the *high* side! I am almost certain that a Deputy Minister would not be half as offended at being called a "Minister", as a full Minister would be at being called a "Deputy Minister"!

Styling of Heads-of-State

Styling of rulers, heirs and consorts

The nine states with royal families style their rulers, heirs to the throne and the official consorts differently. The styling is presented below in a table, showing at a glance what the differences and similarities are.

Styling of Rulers, Heirs and Consorts – Table 1

State	Ruler	Official Consort	Heir to the Throne	Official Consort of Heir to the Throne
Johor	Sultan	Sultanah	Tunku Mahkota	Known by own name. At present Y.A.M. Rajah Zarith Sofiah bte Almarhum Sultan Idris Shah
Kedah	Sultan	Sultanah	Raja Muda	Raja Puan Muda
Kelantan	Sultan	Raja Perempuan	Tengku Mahkota (not married)	
Negeri Sembilan	Yang Di Pertuan Besar	Tunku Ampuan	Please see explanation on page 76	
Pahang	Sultan	Tengku Ampuan, if she is of royal linage. At present, Sultanah Pahang	Tengku Mahkota	Tengku Puan Pahang
Perak	Sultan	Raja Perempuan, if she is of royal lineage. At present, Raja Permaisuri	Raja Muda (not married) Please see explanation on page 77	

State	Ruler	Official Consort	Heir to the Throne	Official Consort of Heir to the Throne
Perlis	Raja	Raja Perempuan	Raja Muda	Raja Puan Muda
Selangor	Sultan	Tengku Ampuan, if she is royal lineage. At present, Che Puan Besar Selangor	Raja Muda	Raja Puan Muda, if of royal lineage. At present known by own name, Y.M. Puan Nurlisa Idris bte Abdullah
Tereng-ganu	Sultan	Tengku Ampuan Besar	Yang DiPertuan Muda (not married)	

Explanatory note for Negeri Sembilan:

Ascension to the throne of Negeri Sembilan is usually not automatically from father to son. This is an elected post among four senior members of the royal family known as the Putera Yang Empat (the Four Royal Children).

The Putera Yang Empat are:

1. The Tunku Besar Sri Menanti
2. The Tunku Laxmana
3. The Tunku Muda Serting
4. The Tunku Panglima Besar

On the death of the ruler, a body that elects the next one (this body is known as the Dato' Undang Yang Empat or the Four Law Givers) meets and elects the new Yang DiPertuan Besar from among these Four Royal Children. In order of priority, this is usually as follows:

1. Sons of the ruler
2. Brothers of the ruler
3. Uncles of the ruler
4. Sons of the ruler's brothers
5. Sons of the ruler's uncle
6. Other senior royal children

Thus, there is no post of Crown Prince/Heir to the Throne in the state of Negeri Sembilan. The ruler himself, not called a Sultan, is styled Yang DiPertuan Besar (He Who is Made Big Lord) for the reasons explained above.

Explanatory note for Perak:
When a Sultan of Perak dies, his son does not automatically succeed him. From as for back as 1786, the descendants of Sultan Ahmaddin Shah (the 18th Sultan of Perak) have been taking turns to be the ruler of Perak.

However, unlike in Negeri Sembilan where any of the four Putera Yang Empat can be elected, the process of succession to the throne of Perak is almost definite, i.e. the prince holding the office of Raja Muda usually ascends the throne on the death of a Sultan.

Among the descendants of Sultan Ahmaddin Shah (three families, as he had three sons), princes are installed in order of ascending seniority as follows:
(starting at No. 1 and ending up at No. 6 as the Raja Muda, the most senior position after the office of Sultan).

1. The Raja Kecil Bongsu
2. The Raja Kecil Tengah
3. The Raja Kecil Sulong
4. The Raja Kecil Besar
5. The Raja DiHilir
6. The Raja Muda

When the Raja Muda becomes Sultan, the Raja DiHilir is promoted to the office of Raja Muda, the Raja Kecil Besar is promoted to the office of the Raja DiHilir, and so on.

The post of Raja Kecil Bongsu would then become vacant and the new Sultan would have to appoint a new Raja

Kecil Bongsu among the princes who are deemed eligible (from the three existing families). Exceptions to this order of succession have been known to happen due to illness or other unusual circumstances.

Styling of governors and consorts

Unlike the nine rulers who ascend the state thrones either by hereditary means or by rotation, the governors are appointed by the Government for a four-year period. While he is in office, a governor takes on the role and the responsibility of a Head-of-State. Governors are entitled to the honorific of Tuan Yang Terutama. The official consort of the governor is given the honorific of Yang Amat Berbahagia whether she is titled or not. This is a courtesy extended to her for being the First Lady in her own state. Honorifics for the other appointed offices are given in Table 5.

Styling of Governors and Consorts – Table 2

State	Governor	Official Consort
Melaka	Yang DiPertua Negeri	By her own title and/or name
Penang	Yang DiPertua Negeri	By her own title and/or name
Sabah	Yang DiPertua Negeri	By her own title and/or name
Sarawak	Yang DiPertua Negeri	By her own title and/or name

Titles, Ranks and Offices

If I were to list all the titles, ranks and offices that exist in Malaysia today, this list would probably be endless. For the purpose of this book, I will include those titles, ranks and offices which you ought to be familiar with while living in the Federal Territory as well as those which should be useful when visiting the rest of Malaysia.

I have listed these titles, ranks and offices along with their appropriate honorific as well as their English equivalent and presented them in tables. Start a row at a time for each table. To get a general idea, read the English equivalent. For example, His Majesty the King would be Duli Yang Maha Mulia Seri Paduka Baginda Yang DiPertuan Agong.

Royal Titles and Ranks

These are the hereditary titles and ranks of the nine royal families in Malaysia.

Royal Titles and Ranks - Table 3 (Correct as of 1991)

Honorific	English Equivalent	Title/Rank	English Equivalent
Duli Yang Maha Mulia Seri Paduka Baginda	His Majesty	Yang DiPertuan Agong	The King (He Who is Made Supreme Ruler)
Duli Yang Maha Mulia Seri Paduka Baginda	Her Majesty	Raja Permaisuri Agong	The Queen (Consort of He Who is Made Supreme Ruler)
Duli Yang Maha Mulia	His Royal Highness	Sultan, Raja, Yang DiPertuan Besar	Head-of-State
Duli Yang Maha Mulia (Note: in some states "Kebawah" is put before Duli Yang Maha Mulia. In this context it means "At the feet of Royalty")	Her Royal Highness	Sultanah, Raja Perempuan, Tengku Ampuan	The Official Consort of the Head-of-State

Honorific	English Equivalent	Title/Rank	English Equivalent
Duli Yang Teramat Mulia/ Duli Yang Amat Mulia/ Yang Teramat Mulia	Literally "The Most Noble/ Illustrious/ Glorious". When used for immediate family members of the ruler, may be translated as His/Her Highness or His/Her Royal Highness	Tengku/ Tunku Mahkota, Raja Muda, Yang DiPertuan Muda	The Crown Prince (Heir to the Throne)
Duli Yang Teramat Mulia/ Yang Teramat Mulia/ Yang Amat Mulia/ Yang Mulia	His/Her Highness or His/Her Royal Highness	Raja Puan Muda, Tengku Puan Pahang and Consorts of Tunku Mahkota of Johor and Raja Muda of Selangor	The Official Consort of the Heir to the Throne
Yang Amat Mulia (only for children of Rulers)	His/Her Highness or His/Her Royal Highness	Tengku/ Tunku, Raja, Syed and Sharifah (Perlis Royal Family only)	Prince/ Princess
Yang Amat Mulia (for Titled Royalty)	His/Her Highness or His/Her Royal Highness	Raja-Raja Bergelar e.g. Tengku Bendahara, Tengku Temenggong, Tengku Laksamana, Tengku Panglima	Titled Royalty
Yang Mulia (for all other members of royal families and some spouses of princes)	His/Her Highness or His/Her Royal Highness	Tengku/ Tunku, Raja, Syed and Sharifah (Perlis Royal Family and some other states)	Member of royal family

Non-Royal Titles and Ranks

Non-royal titles and ranks are conferred on individuals either by the Federal Government, by the Governors or by the Royal Heads-of-State.

Non-Royal Titles and Ranks – Table 4

Honorific	English Equivalent	Title/Rank	English Equivalent
Yang Amat Berbahagia	The Most Fortunate	Tun and Toh Puan (wife of a Tun)	Sir and Lady
Yang Berbahagia (Y.Bhg. and *not* Y.B. which is for Yang Berhormat)	The Fortunate	Tan Sri and Puan Sri (wife of a Tan Sri); Datuk/Dato' and Datin, Tok Puan (wife of a Datuk/Dato')	Sir and Lady

Appointed Offices

These are offices in the Federal Government, the State Governments, the Civil Service, the Diplomatic Service and the Judicial Service.

Appointed Offices – Table 5

Honorific	English Equivalent	Office
Tuan Yang Terutama	His Excellency	Governors, High Commissioners and Ambassadors
Yang Amat Berhormat	The Most Honourable	The Prime Minister, The Deputy Prime Minister, The Chief Minister
Yang Berhormat (Y.B.)	The Honourable	Members of Parliament
Yang Amat Ariff	The Most Learned	The Lord President, The Chief Justice
Yang Ariff	The Learned	Other Judges

While in office which carries an honorific (given to a person by virtue of his holding that particular office) this person is to be addressed by his office honorific e.g. if a Datuk happens to be a Minister, he would take the honorific of Yang Berhormat, which is the honorific given to the office of a Minister. However, when this Datuk retires or leaves his office, he takes on the honorific of Yang Berbahagia which is the honorific given to all Datuks.

Religious Titles

Mufti	– an official who assists a judge by formal exposition of the religious laws.
Kadhi	– a religious officer.
Imam	– a priest
Haji (feminine: Hajjah)	– a person who has performed the full pilgrimage in the Holy Land.
Ustaz (feminine: Ustazah)	– a religious teacher.

For all the above, the courteous Tuan (feminine: Puan) is to be affixed. In some states the honorific Yang Mulia is also accorded, e.g. Yang Mulia Tuan Mufti.

Syed (feminine: Sharifah)	– the only religious title a person is born with.

It is generally accepted here in Malaysia that a Syed is a direct descendant of our Prophet Muhammad (S.A.W.), therefore qualifying it as a religious title. As with the above religious titles, the courteous Tuan (feminine: Puan) is the correct form of address for *all* Syeds and Sharifahs regardless of the fact that they are not married or still very young e.g. an unmarried Sharifah is still to be addressed as Puan Sharifah So-and-So, and a young Syed (even if he is two years old) is still to be addressed as Tuan Syed So-and-So.

The Perlis royal family

Without going into intricate historical detail, I should mention that the princes from the state of Perlis are Syeds. So in this case, the Syed used for the Perlis royal family is not only a religious title but a royal title as well.

The Ruler has seen fit to maintain the title of Syed rather than adopting the Malay word for prince (Tengku/Tunku), making it very important that you remember to address members of the Perlis royal family in exactly the same way you would address other Malay royalty. You would use the honorific of Yang Amat Mulia for the children of the Ruler and Yang Mulia for other members of this family.

How does one tell a Royal Syed from the other Syeds? Apart from knowing that particular Syed's family history, one really cannot. However, the Perlis royal family carries the family name of Jamalullail. So, if you were to be introduced to such a Syed, chances are he is a Perlis prince.

Note: Some other states (e.g. Kedah) have also conferred royal status on Syeds, therefore they get the honorific of Yang Mulia and are spoken to in Royal Malay.

Spelling Differences

Is there a difference between a...

- Tengku and a Tunku?

None. Except for the spelling, which tells you which royal family the Tengku/Tunku belongs to.

- Toh Puan and a Tok Puan?

Yes. A Toh Puan with an 'h' is the wife of a Tun. A Tok Puan with a 'k' is the wife of a Dato' from Terengganu and a hereditary Dato' from Pahang. The title Tok Puan is derived from Datok Perempuan (feminine/spouse of Dato').

- Datuk and a Dato'?

Yes. A Datuk is a person who received his Datukship from the Federal Government or from states that are headed by Governors (Melaka, Penang, Sabah and Sarawak). A Dato' is one who received his Dato'ship from a Royal Head-of-State.

- And who is a Datin Paduka?

She is a lady who has been conferred the title of Dato' in her own right (Selangor). To complicate matters, she could *also* be the wife of a Datuk Paduka (a Datukship received from the state of Melaka).

How do you tell whether a lady is a Dato' in her own right or the wife of a Datuk Paduka? Verbally, you cannot. You might have to ask her personally.

Verbal Address
Formal Verbal Address
- The Rulers, their Official Consorts, the Crown Princes (Heirs to the Throne): Tuanku
- The Official Consorts of the Crown Princes (Heirs to the Throne): Ku Puan or by name (Johor and Selangor)
- Members of the Royal Families: Tengku/Tunku

The collective Malay word for prince is Tengku/Tunku. Therefore, in conversation, it is completely acceptable that you call a Malay prince Tengku/Tunku, even though he may be Raja (Perak) or Syed (Perlis only).

Spouses of members of royal families
Malaysia must be the only country left in the world where morganatic marriages (a marriage between a prince and a commoner where the wife is not elevated to the rank of princess) still exist.

Whether the wife of a prince is to be given semi or full royal status is completely up to the Ruler concerned. Some states have been doing this for years, others are doing it now, but whatever the case may be, a lady marrying into the royal family does not become a princess automatically.

A title, that was traditionally a courteous one, has now been gazetted officially in many states as an honorary title for non-royal wives who marry senior royalty. This title supersedes any other title(s) [like Toh Puan, Puan Sri, or Datin] that existed before as it is somewhat on-par with the royal title of Tengku. Just as a Tengku would be known as Tengku

Datin So-and-so, a Che Puan would also be known as Che Puan So-and-so.

In the state of Negeri Sembilan, the official honorary title for non-royal wives who marry senior royalty is Che Engku. Unless otherwise stated, all wives who have the titles of Tengku, Che Puan or Che Engku, all enjoy the same rank and status as each other, according to their husband's rank and status.

Dato's/Datuks

Seeing that there are many variations of the title Dato'/Datuk (Patinggi/Seri/Paduka, etc), it is considered acceptable that you refer verbally to all Dato's/Datuks as Dato'/Datuk without necessarily having to add the Patinggi/Seri/Paduka, etc.

More than one title

Although there are no hard-and-fast rules as to how a person with more than one title should be addressed (the most senior title usually takes precedence) the order in which his title(s)/rank/name are written down is normally done as follows:

More Than One Title – Table 6

Honorific	Professional Title	Royal Title	Title(s) Bestowed by Head-of-State	Religious Title	Name
Yang Mulia	Major General	Tengku	Dato'	Haji	Ahmad
Yang Berbahagia	Professor		Tan Sri/ Dato'		Ahmad

Although his professional title comes first, his honorific is still taken from his royal title. Thus Tengku Ahmad's full name should read: Yang Mulia Major General Tengku Dato' Haji Ahmad.

Professor Ahmad takes his honorific from his Tan Sriship/ Dato'ship (usually Federal awards take precedence over state awards in the Federal Territory). Thus, his full name should read: Yang Berbahagia Professor Tan Sri Dato' Ahmad.

Royal Malay

There are certain Malay words and terms which are used only for those occasions when one converses with members of the royal families. We call this royal Malay. The main emphasis of royal Malay is in the way it is spoken and the way various movements of the hands and body accompany one's conversation. This is not easy and it takes a lot of experience and practice before a person can master the art of conversing in royal Malay.

While foreigners are not expected to know royal Malay, royalty is always happy (and impressed) when foreigners use some of these royal terms when speaking with them. There are certain words, especially pronouns such as "I", "me" and "you", which can be substituted with royal Malay words. For example, the sentence "I would be most honoured if you (referring to the royal person) would accept this small gift from me" would become "Patik (I) would be most honoured if Tuanku (for rulers, their official consorts and heirs to the throne) or Tengku (for other members of royal families) would accept this small gift from patik (me)". If you were asked a question such as "Do you live in Kuala Lumpur?", and your answer was "Yes, I live in Kuala Lumpur", using royal Malay, your answer would be "Tuanku, patik lives in Kuala Lumpur".

Some of the more useful royal Malay words – Table 7

English	Bahasa Malaysia	Royal Malay
I/me	Saya	Patik
Yes (when answering)	Saya	Tuanku/Ku
You	Awak	Tuanku/Tengku/Ku
To talk	Cakap	Titah
To eat	Makan	Santap
To drink	Minum	Santap minum
To go/leave	Pergi	Berangkat
To come back/return	Balik/pulang	Berangkat balik/ berangkat pulang

English	Bahasa Malaysia	Royal Malay
To sleep	Tidur	Beradu
To bathe	Mandi	Siram
To give	Beri	Sembah
To tell	Beritahu	Sembah kepada
To take leave of	Minta diri	Mohon
Ill/sick	Sakit	Gering
Angry	Marah/meradang	Murka

It must be strongly emphasised, however, that the modern usage of royal Malay is more out of courtesy than demand, and is very much left to the individual as to whether he feels he can accept these "rules and regulations" which are peculiar only to royal Malay.

Malay names

As we do not have surnames, it is important for non-Malays to remember to call a Malay person by the first name they hear (otherwise they might be calling this person by his father's name instead).

For example, if someone introduces himself as Ahmad Ibrahim, you call him Encik Ahmad and not Encik Ibrahim, as Encik Ibrahim is this gentleman's father's name.

Encik is the Malay term for Mister and is the appropriate form of address when in polite or formal conversation with Malay men. However, referring to a Malay lady is much more confusing.

A Malay lady could introduce herself to you as Aminah Abdullah, for example. Is Abdullah her father's name or her husband's name? Unless this Aminah tells you her life story immediately upon being introduced, there is no way you can tell. It is, however, a common practice among Malay ladies to use their father's name (rather than their husband's name) after their own name. Aminah Abdullah would then be called Puan Aminah.

To make things more confusing, some Malay ladies do follow the Western approach of being Mrs. So-and-So (using their husband's name) and they, then, prefer to be known as

Puan Abdullah, in this example.

Puan is the Malay term for "Madam/Mrs/Wife of" and can be used as a term of respect to unmarried ladies as well. This is the appropriate form of address when in polite or formal conversation with Malay ladies. Although Cik is the Malay term for Miss, when in doubt over a woman's marital status, I would suggest you opt for *Puan*. It does, after all, not only include all married ladies but respected unmarried ladies as well.

A foreigner is bound to come across a Malay person's name with the word *bin* or *binti* inserted between the first name and the second name. For example, Encik Ahmad bin Ibrahim or Puan Aminah binti Abdullah. *Bin* is the Arabic term for "Son of" and *binti* is the Arabic term for "Daughter of" and we, being Muslims, have adopted this styling.

Not all Malay ladies who use their father's name include the word *binti*. Since there are no hard-and-fast rules governing the use of *binti,* it is safer to assume that the second name you hear, in this example Abdullah, is the father's name and not the husband's name.

Nik, Wan and Megat (feminine: Putri)

There is some confusion as to what Nik, Wan and Megat are. Are they names or titles? In Malaysia, both views are held. If a person holds the view that Nik, Wan and Megat are clan or family names then he should be addressed as Encik Nik, Encik Wan or Encik Megat depending on which of the three he belongs to. On the other hand, if a person called Nik, Wan or Megat holds the view that these terms are semi-royal titles where royalty is on the maternal side, then the correct way to address this person is without the Encik in front.

How do you tell one type of Nik, Wan or Megat from the other? Apart from checking with him personally, I don't think there is a clear-cut answer to this question.

Non-Malay names

Like the Malays, Southern Indians also do not have surnames and the correct way to address them would be in the same way as for the Malays. Some of the Northern Indians have family names and they can be addressed in the Western way. Sikhs have a common surname for all men and another for women. Men should be addressed as Mr. Singh and married ladies as Mrs. Singh; unmarried ladies should be addressed as Miss Kaur. Some Sikhs adopt a particular name for a family name and they may prefer to be addressed according to the family name instead of the surnames of Singh or Kaur.

The Chinese usually put their surnames in front of their given names. Thus Mr. Lim Chin Swee, for example, would be Mr. Lim. If you were a close friend, you would call him Chin Swee. The Chinese usually have two given names though some have only one.

Informal verbal address

Having just arrived in Malaysia, a European friend of mine told me that she was completely taken aback when her daughter's little Malaysian friend called her "auntie". While my friend could understand that auntie may be used to call someone your parents are very close to (e.g., your mother's best friend), she felt it extremely strange that a little girl she had never met before should refer to her in such a familiar way.

Not surprisingly, she nearly had a heart attack when her elderly gardener began to call her "auntie" as well.

In the English language, there are only two forms of address: formal (e.g. Mrs. Jones) and informal (e.g. Tom). While it may be completely acceptable for young people in the West to call their older friends by their first names, over here this is not the case. Such familiarity is strongly discouraged and is generally frowned upon. Neither do we feel that it is appropriate for our children's friends to call us Mrs. So-and-So. This is too formal.

Thus we use such terms as *datuk* (grandfather), *nenek* (grandmother), *pakcik* (uncle), *makcik* (auntie), *abang* (older brother), *kakak* (older sister) and *adik* (younger brother or sister) when both the Western formal and informal forms of address are inappropriate. These in-between forms of address show a great deal of respect to people especially when we do not know their names, ages or titles. They are, after all, terms of endearment; as if we all belong to one family.

But why did the elderly gardener call my friend "auntie" as well? In this case it was out of respect and submission from an employee to an employer, even though the employee is much older in age.

You will also find that our children are encouraged to call family staff (nanny, cook, driver, etc.) by this in-between form of address.

At this point, I must stress that non-Malays also have their own equivalents of this one-family form of address. You will find that the Chinese, the Indians and the Eurasians often refer to people older than themselves as uncle, auntie, brother or sister in their own languages or dialects or even in the English language. English is often used when two Malaysians belonging to two different ethnic groups converse with each other.

Foreigners might as well get used to this particular type of address, as you are bound to be "auntie-d" or "uncle-d" more times than you can remember during your stay here in Malaysia!

EPILOGUE

I do hope what the reader has read so far has been of some constructive use to him or her. I also hope that, after putting all the guidelines and tips from the book into practice, the reader will not only have a deeper understanding of Malaysian customs and etiquette but also greater confidence when interacting with the people of Malaysia.

My final word of advice is: after having read the book from cover to cover, and you still cannot get rid of this nagging worry that you might still commit a local *faux pas*, nothing works better than a profuse apology *in advance* to the person you may offend. In this way, even though you may proceed to blunder outrageously, at least you have already asked to be forgiven!

BIBLIOGRAPHY

Abdullah Ali (1986), *Malaysian Protocol and Correct Forms of Address*, Times Books International, Malaysia.

Information Malaysia 1990-91 Yearbook, Berita Publishing, Malaysia.

Mochtar bin Haji Md Dom, Haji (1979), *Malay Superstitions and Beliefs*, Federal Publications, Malaysia.

Ryan, N.J. (1985), *The Cultural Heritage of Malaya*, Longman Malaysia, Malaysia.

Sheppard, M. (1981), *Malay Courtesy*, Eastern Universities Press, Malaysia.

Walters, D. (1988), *Cast Your Chinese Horoscope*, Asiapac Books, Singapore.

ABOUT THE AUTHOR

Datin Noor Aini began writing while she was still at school. After completing her matriculations in Singapore, she attended the Institute of Tourism and Hotel Management in Salzburg, Austria. Upon obtaining her diploma in Tourism, Datin Noor Aini joined the Centre of Economic and Political Studies in London, England. She graduated in June 1979.

Before leaving for Kuala Lumpur, she worked with the Malaysian Tourist Office (TDC) in London. During the one year that she spent there she was often asked to give talks on Malaysia. She also contributed several articles on Malaysia which were published in the trade publications distributed among the members of the tourist trade.

Between 1981 to 1984 she wrote on a freelance basis for a Singapore based fashion magazine.

Datin Noor Aini is the youngest child of Ambassador Datuk Abdullah bin Ali, a retired diplomat and author of the book *Malaysian Protocol and Correct Forms of Address*. Since 1985, together with her father, Datin Noor Aini has participated in many seminars and has been giving talks on subjects related to Malaysian protocol, Malaysian etiquette and manners, and basic traditional Malaysian customs and culture.

In 1988, Datin Noor Aini wrote her first book *Jadilah Wanita Yang Dikagumi* (Becoming a Woman to be Admired) which was quickly proclaimed a national bestseller. Later that same year, this book achieved fame as a bestseller at the Kuala Lumpur Festival of Books; it also won an award in the Best Designed Book – Adult section at the Singapore Festival of Books.

Datin Noor Aini is a member of the Perlis royal family through her marriage to Yang Amat Mulia Syed Amir Abidin ibni Tuanku Syed Putra Jamalullail, third son of Duli-Duli Yang Maha Mulia the Raja and Raja Perempuan Perlis Indera Kayangan. She has a daughter, Yang Mulia Sharifah Nurul Afzan Jamalullail. Being the daughter of a diplomat and the wife of a prince allows Datin Noor Aini to gain first-hand knowledge and experience on the subjects in which she now specialises.

During her spare time, she tries to do some charity work. To date she has helped out in the fund-raising activities of the Society for the Severely and Mentally Handicapped, the Selangor Cheshire Home, and also a few charitable institutes in Perlis. Her favourite hobbies are reading, writing and illustrating short stories with her eight-year-old daughter.

Datin Noor Aini Syed Amir with her daughter